WOMEN OF MERCY

WOMEN OF MERCY

KATHY COFFEY

Art by

MICHAEL O'NEILL McGRATH

ORBIS BOOKS

Maryknoll, New York 10545

Founded in 1970, Orbis Books endeavors to publish works that enlighten the mind, nourish the spirit, and challenge the conscience. The publishing arm of the Maryknoll Fathers and Brothers, Orbis seeks to explore the global dimensions of the Christian faith and mission, to invite dialogue with diverse cultures and religious traditions, and to serve the cause of reconciliation and peace. The books published reflect the views of their authors and do not represent the official position of the Maryknoll Society. To learn more about Maryknoll and Orbis Books, please visit our website at www.maryknoll.org.

Library of Congress Cataloging-in-Publication Data

Coffey, Kathy.
   Women of mercy / Kathy Coffey ; with art by Michael O'Neill McGrath.
      p. cm.
   Includes bibliographical references.
   ISBN 1-57075-579-5 (pbk.)
   1. Catholic women—Biography. 2. Catholics—Biography. 3. Christian women saints—Biography. 4. Christian saints—Biography. 5. Women in the Bible—Biography. 6. Bible—Biography. 7. Mercy. I. McGrath, Michael O'Neill. II. Title.
   BX4667.C64 2005
   282'.092'2—dc22

                                                            2004018889

you . . . clung like an acrobat, by your teeth, fiercely,
to a cobweb-thin high-wire, your certainty
of infinite mercy, witnessed
with your own eyes . . .

—Denise Levertov, "The Showings:
Lady Julian of Norwich"

Contents

Contents

Introduction

One word sings across the centuries, the word for which the human heart longs: mercy. The divine care is cupped in human hands, etched in the lines of human lives. Michael McGrath has given this quality of mercy a human face. His art creates a sisterhood of merciful mamas to watch over growing girls. This community crisscrosses time, united by one hand outstretched, one strength as firm as cedar yet lithe enough to lean through intervening years and touch us.

A searching teenager can find in this family portrait the inspiration for all she will someday be. A weary older woman can catch from these animated conversations a rekindling spark. The community of these women surpasses the cozy zone of intimate friends. Their circle gives more than comfort. It brings an empowering sense that we can change this world together, one small bit at a time.

What Is Mercy?

The quality of mercy is not strained. Neither is it easily defined. Perhaps an understanding comes through the sketched line of a woman's shoulder, bending in empathy. Or appreciation is shaped by story:

Once a girl named Catherine walked out the door of a Dublin home. She saw misery in its slums and intervened. This servant or that orphan needed shelter. Mercy prompted her to see with sympathetic eyes and act with generous heart.

Another young Katharine saw the open sores of Native Americans. Her heart went out to them—as did her fortune. What propelled her? We name it mercy.

Nothing we can say of this virtue will ever be complete. Ultimately it cannot be pinned down because it must live on in the efforts of human beings today. A visual image for that continuing work appears at Old St. Patrick's Church in Chicago, where statues of saints surround the perimeter. Near St. Brigid and her cow stands an empty niche, reserved for anyone people imagine there. It may be someone they revere; on better days it may be themselves. So too, readers can imagine here one blank page. On it they can insert someone they admire—or themselves.

Why learn the ancestral history of the merciful? Our culture cheers the merciless, whose knife blade flashes swift and sharp. Harsh headlines scream, "No Mercy!" Heroes obsessed with being "cool" deny the mercy we desire. Learning the ways of the large-hearted seems countercultural, slightly subversive. Yet who contributed more to human happiness: the tyrants who slaughtered or the nurses who saved lives?

The Process

Brother Mickey McGrath designed the "Women of Mercy" for Merion Mercy Academy near Philadelphia. True to the dynamic of merciful women, he did not work alone. The whole high school got involved: faculty members and students, theologians and artists. The young women who studied the inspiring women in theology classes painted them in art.

Their work, hanging on the chapel walls, gifts future generations. As students fret over SAT scores, eating disorders, algebra, soccer, a friend's addiction, aging grandparents, and prom dates, the presence of these women reminds them of even larger issues, such as how they're sharpening their skills to fight injustice or why God put them on the planet.

There is nothing like a heroic woman to put teenage—or midlife—anxiety into perspective. "It's about more than you, darlin'," she whispers sweetly to those trapped in narrowness or self-pity. In "The Mercy of God," poet Jessica Powers described this setting-aside-of-self to enter mercy:

> I rose up from the acres of self that I tended with passion
>   and defended with flurries of pride;
> I walked out of myself and went into the woods of God's
>   mercy,
> and here I abide.

The girls attest that everyone wanted to get in on the act. When something truly creative and positive is happening, no one wants to be left behind. They are justifiably proud of themselves: "We could never make a mistake. Everything, every stroke of paint, every swirl of gesso, was beautiful to Brother Mickey!" (May Limbach). Jessica Mercer pays the ultimate compliment: "I was compelled to even stay after school for a few hours to lend a hand."

One suspects that when the young artists are old as Sarah, they'll bring great-grandchildren to see their work: "When I was sixteen, I painted those crosses on Tekakwitha." Caitlin Rice confirms the suspicion: "Years from now I can proudly say that I painted the face of Veronica who wiped the face of Jesus!"

One likes to imagine Caitlin, the kind of girl who hates to see the project end. "Each day I anxiously awaited art class and taking part in this great project." But she probably knows the project never ends. The work of mercy is simply transferred from canvas to her own life. Privileged to play a part in the grand design, she or one of the other young artists/theologians will be the next Dorothy Day. The world awaits her with desperate hunger.

The young artists move daily, as all do, past neon signs, through airwaves cluttered with smut, advertising, and Internet sites that exploit women's bodies. They wonder where they'll fit into a tight economy and a job market that's laying off their parents. But they also walk with the confidence that they have created something enduring and beautiful which opens the door to the sacred. They can hear within the whisper of merciful women: "Go and do likewise. Become like us."

No one comes to the National Gallery to find beauty only within its walls. People visiting art museums become sensitized to beauty there, then find it everywhere. So too, readers meeting mercy in these portraits painted in acrylic and words seek mercy everywhere. That lovely quality emerges in the people they encounter, the chances they have to give and receive mercy.

The girls' hands-on learning won't be forgotten: "Painting the women was cool but messy. The gold is still glowing in my hands!" (Kerry McCarthy). It is also a potent reminder of women's synergy in a church and society that ignore feminine gifts at their peril. These girls will never doubt the power of a committed female. "Sometimes it seems like the female role in Christian history is diminished, but it was reassuring to be reminded of all these amazing women and their accomplishments" (Katelyn Moscony).

All the merciful deeds of all these women added together might give the merest glimpse into the ocean of God's mercy. A phrase from Thomas Merton captures the eternal echo within the space these women create: "Mercy within mercy within mercy."

The Pattern

In the belief that one shortcut to truth is a story, a parable in Luke's Gospel describes the work of mercy. The women are like God, and in a lovely circle, God is like the woman who loses her coin, lights her lamp, sweeps her house, finds it, and celebrates. We can interpret the coin as a person, lost in the wreckage of war or tossed aside by the Industrial Age. Then we can see the parallel between the woman Jesus describes and some of the merciful women.

Or what woman having ten coins and losing one would not
- *light* a lamp and
- *sweep* the house, *searching* carefully until she finds it?
- And when she does *find* it,
- she calls together her friends and neighbors and says to them, "*Rejoice* with me because I have found the coin that was lost." (Luke 15:8-10)

Let's look at each action:

She *lights* the lamp because she needs keen vision in a dark house. Mercy must reach into the shadowy corners and deep canyons of human evil. She focuses on Jesus, who sought the lost sheep, representing the most marginalized people of his society. She identifies so strongly with Jesus that Catherine of Siena imagined God telling her, "You are another myself."

The inner life fuels the external action. Jesus promised, "You shall do greater things than I," and she takes his promise seriously. Because of this solidarity, she can act like God's daughter, filled with grace and strength, rising to impossible challenges. That's why Thea Bowman could persuade the American bishops to link arms and sing "We Shall Overcome," or Katharine Drexel could educate the Native Americans and African Americans whom everyone else ignored.

"Come, let us walk in the light of the Lord!" wrote the prophet Isaiah (2:5). Catherine of Siena echoed: "What a marvelous thing that even while we are in the dark we should know the light."

She *sweeps* the house, energetically clearing the clutter. She doesn't simply forget the coin, vaguely hoping that it might emerge the next day. She grabs the broom because she's upset and angry, convinced that the coin (or the person) is precious. An earthy vein of practicality runs through the parable and through these women's lives. They don't simply organize committees or speculate about the problem—they DO something.

They move briskly from religion-as-reassurance to faith-as-imperative to transform the world. They operate out of "the conviction that despite all evidence to the contrary, God's spirit of mercy is at work in our world and in our lives, empowering us to be ministers of compassion and healing."[1]

What role does righteous anger play in the works of mercy? Surely it galvanizes some to action. These women make positive use of anger's energy, not wallowing in tragic injustice. Instead of becoming depressed, they tackle the systems that cause the suffering. So Frances Cabrini became a legend with the produce dealers of Denargo Market in Denver. She *told* them (never *begging*) what to load on her truck to feed her orphans. Not just the leftovers or the produce-bordering-on-rot. Nope, the good stuff.

She *searches* carefully, matching the need of a particular time with her particular talent, finding the people who need her most and concentrating on them. So Jesus sought out those who most needed his help and healed them. So Mother Teresa and her sisters combed the streets of Calcutta, seeking the dying or abandoned.

How lovely and important that she *finds* the coin. The story doesn't end sadly because in one sense we are already found. These women draw on a deep pool of forgiveness, saying, "Welcome home no matter what you did," offering everyone the enormous relief of being OK exactly "as is," with no spruce-up improvements.

These women know that their work is a participation in God's, the source of all mercy, who leads them to their work, empowers them to do it, and energizes them for the long haul. Their response to suffering humanity is nothing short of magnificent.

Finally she *rejoices* with her friends and neighbors. The theme recurs throughout these lives: the work itself is a joy. The women feel honored to be doing it. When they encounter tragedy, sadness, and failure, these "glorious girls" return to the wellsprings of joy. "There's a time for fasting and a time for partridges," Teresa of Avila declared. As she dug into the feast, she chortled: "This is the time for partridges!" In case anyone missed the point, she added, "From silly devotions and sour-faced saints, good Lord deliver us!"

Weakened by cancer, Thea Bowman kept singing spirituals. On Saturday afternoon, Dorothy Day listened faithfully to the Metropolitan Opera radio broadcast. Desperately poor, Elizabeth Ann Seton wheedled elegant ball gowns from her friends for her daughter Kit. Without the joyous interludes, the work of mercy might become drudgery, a pallid shroud beside the vibrant colors it should wear.

What, then, does the parable teach us of mercy? Opening the 2004 Los Angeles Religious Education Congress, entitled "Steeped in Mercy, Balm for the World," Sister Edith Prendergast described mercy in terms like those of the parable's "rescue mission." It "reaches into the dark corners, the cracks of our flailing and our faltering. Mercy seeps into that space, picks us up, holds us, and enfolds us in love until we are restored, made whole again." Then we celebrate the restoration; we "taste the cream and quintessence of God's mercies."

The elements of this story parallel similar ones in the parable that follows: the prodigal son. Luke 15:11-32 has the same elements of loss, search (the father goes out of his house to both sons), the practicality of rings, sandals, and fatted calves, the celebration that parallels the angels of heaven rejoicing. Both parables evoke the image of God's lost, beloved child, defeated by poverty, ravaged by disease, or weary from too long a time away from home. As in the Beatitudes, Jesus looks beyond the scruffy appearance of the crowd and sees the deeper blessing. Like Father, like son.

Conclusion—and Beginning

As these portraits were painted, *The Secret Life of Bees* by Sue Monk Kidd was a best-selling novel. McGrath's art could have illustrated its concluding scene of the Daughters of

Mary, stalwart African American women "clutching their pocketbooks . . . like they might have to use them to beat the living hell out of somebody."

They defend Lily the narrator against her abusive father. Their resolve says without a word, "I double dog dare you to take this girl" away from their home. Their moral authority wins the day, and her father gives up and drives off. Lily remembers "the sight of them standing there waiting. All these women, all this love, waiting."

Every girl should have such a wall of women to guard, to cheer, to inspire. Those who don't happen to attend Merion Mercy Academy have this book.

Mary Mother of Mercy

$\mathcal{M}$ary

Mother of Mercy

Pray for the living and the dead

To understand mercy, we begin with Mary: the archetype, mother, and source. If those titles sound off-putting, remember her as a girl. She saw the world pivoting on its hunger, filled with rage, blind to the victims of its brutality. This teenager saw the full horror. Then she said yes to whatever she could do, despite her youth, despite her innocence, to change it.

In Brother Mickey's portrait, Mary's hands are uplifted in an open, iconic *Orans* position, a traditional gesture of prayer. This depiction links to contemporary celebrations that release flocks of doves. She unleashes a whirlwind of energy, shown here in the symbol of the Holy Spirit. Unlike some saccharine, lily-white images of her, Mary is strong, multicultural, her hair an elaborate African braid.

While Mary's whole life is suffused with mercy, three focal points show it well: the visitation, the wedding at Cana, and Jesus' passion.

The Visitation (Luke 1:39-56)

Mary sings her "Magnificat" during a visit to her cousin Elizabeth when both women know they are pregnant. The poem specifically mentions mercy twice.

> God's mercy extends from generation to generation.
> [God] has helped his servant Israel, in remembrance of [God's] mercy.

From Generation to Generation

Mary stands in a long line of foremothers who had experienced astonishing surprises: Miriam, Deborah, Judith, Esther.

Her words parallel Hannah's, who became pregnant after God's gracious intervention with the childless.

Spiritual writers speak of women like Mary creating the "master metaphors" that later generations then adapt to their own times. From the twelfth century onward, Christians have addressed to Mary the Memorare, attributed to St. Bernard of Clairvaux: "in thy mercy hear and answer me."

Mary's timelessness prompted the anguished cry of Gerard Manley Hopkins, a Jesuit poet, almost 1900 years after she lived:

Mary, mother of us, where is your relief?[1]

Hopkins would also find comfort in her:

I saw that we are wound
With mercy round and round
As if with air . . .[2]

"From generation to generation" touches our own day. A grieving Lutheran woman in North Dakota tells Kathleen Norris: "I love Mary, because she also knew what it is to lose a child."[3] Two popular contemporary novels show how Mary continues to mother even abused or neglected children. Rebecca Wells describes such a child in *Divine Secrets of the Ya-Ya Sisterhood:*

> Sidda stands in the moonlight and lets the Blessed Mother love every hair on her 6-year old head. . . . From one fleeting, luminous moment, Sidda Walker knows there has never been a time when she has not been loved.

The Black Madonna, discussed in the "Passion" section of this chapter, is one heroine of *The Secret Life of Bees.* To African American slaves, she represented freedom and consolation. Years later, Lily the narrator, abandoned by her mother, longs to touch the statue for the consolation it had offered people before her. Her yearning parallels Teresa of Avila's, whose mother died when she was twelve. Turning to Mary, Teresa says simply, "in the end she brought me back to myself."

Lily could be describing Brother Mickey's portrait: "Her eyes were mysterious and kind and her skin dark brown with a glow, darker than toast and looking a little like it had been buttered." "I thought of Mary's spirit, hidden everywhere. Her heart a red cup of fierceness tucked among ordinary things"—or a vessel filled with flame.

More important than Mary's appearance is the way she empowers Lily to "live like the glorious girl you are." As a wise mentor explains, "Our Lady is not some magical being out there somewhere, like a fairy godmother. . . . She's something *inside* of you. . . . You have to find a mother inside yourself. . . . Even if we already have a mother, we still have to find this part of ourselves inside." "This Mary I'm talking about sits in your heart all day long, saying, 'Lily, you are my everlasting home. Don't you ever be afraid. I am enough. We are enough.'"[4]

A Mercifully Active God

Art that depicts the Pietà, Mary cradling her dead son on her lap, reminds people that daily care for others, especially the sick and dying, is care for Christ. Women like Frances Cabrini or Catherine McAuley would enact this mercy in concrete responses to specific needs. During the nineteenth century,

God's people take on the face of an Italian orphan in New York or a servant fired in Dublin. Like the women in this book, she is actively engaged, *not* the passive, sweet figure some religious art suggests.

When Jesus praised the woman who found the lost coin, did he remember Mary? As a boy, he must have heard her exuberant celebration in the "Magnificat." She is completely caught up in joy, not one who begrudges God some half-hearted thanks. The identity she has found transcends her low status in society. No mere girl, she is the partner of God, and together they will do great things. Despite the struggles ahead, the angel called an "insignificant" peasant "highly favored" and invited her to rejoice. Hard to refuse *that* invitation!

Just as Jesus' knowledge of the Father inspires his whole outlook and ministry, so Mary trusts God completely and finds her delight in God. She becomes the first "spokeswoman for God's redemptive justice," and Jesus becomes the "mother lode of God's life-giving mercy for the world."[5] To Mary, the divine compassion is no pious abstraction, but a matter of forthright deeds. In her "Magnificat" vision, God's active mercy lifts up the poor and overthrows the oppressive. This revolutionary woman uses active verbs: *scatter* (the proud), *pull down* (the powerful), *send away* (the rich). Her canticle prefigures the Beatitudes, which became the mission statement for many merciful women.

Anyone who has ever felt lonely, debased, disempowered, or abandoned can look with hope to Mary's words. She announces a new order: God will not tolerate the degradation or destruction of a single one of God's precious creatures. We who have grown overly familiar with the "Magnificat" forget how subversive it can be. During the 1980s, the Guatemalan regime forbade the singing of it in public. For those who are cozy with the way things are: beware. It points not only to the uplifting of the poor but to the transformation of the rich. God takes mercy on a suffering world and sends us *all* to make it better.

Mary embodies this new order because God hasn't chosen a princess or a priestess for Jesus' mother. In choosing Mary, God has affirmed every woman who struggles to feed her family, protect her children, beautify her world, and bring hope into the ruins. Mary says yes to God, but she also says no to injustice, as Catherine of Siena later would: "Enough. This cannot continue." Flames surround her portrait because the polarities of warming and destroying are both embraced by symbol.

The God of Jesus sounds familiar; then you realize this is the God of Mary. It seems safe to assume he learned to pray from her. So the echoes of "fill the starving with good things" resonate in "give us this day our daily bread." In the thirteenth century, Richard of St. Laurent made the allusion specific: "Our mother who art in heaven, give us our daily bread."[6] Contemporary Jesuit Joseph Brown says, "There is a whole lot of 'Our Mama' in the 'Our Father.'"[7] The God of Jesus and Mary is a motherly chef who cooks the best recipes for the hungriest kids.

It would be understandable if Mary saw God as distant, punitive, or angry. After all, she lived in a small village under Roman oppression and wasn't highly educated. She didn't see much liberation—of women or anyone else. She was prophetic to envision the reign of justice so boldly. How could those who followed *not* get caught up in the "Magnificat's" heartening vision?

The Wedding at Cana (John 2:1-11)

Mary's bold, original plan would spill over into actions of her later life. She doesn't seem bothered by social taboos against women's initiatives when she steps in to solve the crisis at a wedding gone suddenly "dry." As historian Henry Adams wrote, "The people loved Mary because she trampled on conventions; not merely because she could do it, but because she liked to do what shocked every well-regulated authority. Her pity had no limit."[8]

When she voiced the obvious need, she not only pointed out, "They have no wine." She reminded the partyers of an economic situation they were probably trying to forget. Their daily lot was scarcity, but her intervention turns it to abundance.

Ignoring her son's reluctance, she displays the vein of practicality that runs throughout the women who follow in these pages. She names the need, organizes the servants, and, in good Jewish-mama style, gives them their marching orders. It isn't hard to imagine her savoring a glass of burgundy herself, joining merrily in the celebration that hadn't ended, but only paused.

Author Elizabeth Johnson applies Mary's words to current global needs. "They have no wine" can translate to: no housing, no education, no dignity, no clean water, no opportunity, no health care. In some churches, a male clerical system that restricts women's God-given gifts may ultimately deprive the people of sacraments. "Mary's strong impulse to call for relief corresponds to God's own dearest desire."[9]

"Do whatever he tells you" directs followers more to doing works of mercy than to honoring any culturally determined laws or time-bound customs. Mary is larger than one box— the world's art has portrayed her as young/old/Asian/ African/European/South American/Jewish/Palestinian.

The Passion (John 19:25-27)

Throughout her life, Mary refused to let legitimate anger consume her energy. Never is this more clear than in the passion narrative, interpreted by two contemporary theologians. Acknowledging that the fourth station of the cross—Jesus meets his mother—is legendary, not scriptural, Beatrice Bruteau explores its symbolic value. "The Blessed Mother means some graciousness of God *in me.*" This ground of being nurtures the spiritual life and guards embryonic desires. The "inner Mary," this "deep source of life and protection," gives strength for the struggle. The "Holy Mother at the foundation of our self" is full of grace.[10]

Ronald Rolheiser points out in *The Holy Longing* that when Mary stands on Calvary the word "stands" represents a position of strength. She doesn't faint, as some artists suggest. Instead, she does exactly what her son does: transforms the pain and the brutality and the ugliness so they do not give it back in kind. She is the same unflinching woman who proclaimed the "Magnificat"—nothing pious or syrupy about her.

She drew her strength, as all must, from her son—and in turn gave him her support. Betsie Ten Boom wrote from her own Calvary of a Nazi concentration camp: "We must tell the people what we have heard here. We must tell them that there is no pit so deep that [God] is not deeper still."

Because she has suffered ultimate loss, Mary knows the suffering of others. Examples from two different cultures affirm her empathy. Father Virgil Elizondo, an authority on Mexican spirituality, describes belief in Our Lady of Guadalupe: "When no one else understood, she understood." An Italian-American who had lost her son would nod her head over and over, repeating, *"Madonna capisce,"* "Mary understands."

Their instincts accord with peoples' responses to the Black Madonna from the Middle Ages on. These popular black statues were carried in procession so that people could hold up their sick children to Mary or ask her help in childbirth and conception. The madonna's large hands suggest her peasant origins, attuned to the daily realities of nature, crops, and illness. She gazes into the distance, perhaps looking beyond immediate suffering to immense joy. Through her face, writes French philosopher André Malraux, "God calls out to humanity sorrow by sorrow." [11]

To Mary at the foot of the cross, split with sorrow, Jesus extends one last mercy. According to John's Gospel, he places her and the beloved disciple into each other's care. Her ultimate heartbreak must have been her inability to soothe his awful torment. Knowing their terrible aloneness, Jesus entrusts her and his friend to each other, to be healed and to heal.

In doing so, he gives the mother of mercy to us and us to her. She becomes a channel of the endless ocean of mercy that washes the cross, cleanses the death camp, and bathes us today. Then she brings a sureness to the step, an energy to the work, a lightness to the touch, and a confidence that mercy is no frail thing.

$\int$arah

Mercy as Mirth

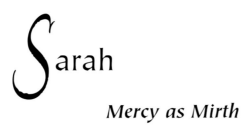

Shelter the homeless

Sarai sheltered angels—that was the easy part. The tough part was housing Abraham, that visionary but often pigheaded patriarch who must have made her wish at times for a larger tent. While we can't expect the old boy to be a feminist, his lies designed to win favor with rulers appall even the pagan kings of his time. When they're new in town, he tells Sarai to pretend she is his sister, concealing her true identity as his wife. Despite the fact that his deception fails with Pharaoh (Gen. 12:19), he tries it again to impress Abimelech (Gen. 20:2). His sneaky advice to Sarai, "Say you are my sister, so that it may go well with *me*," must be some ultimate oxymoron, a teetering pillar of male insecurity.

Hostility to Hagar

The fact that Abram treated Sarai like a piece of furniture or an ox to be bartered in self-protection must have spilled over into her own treatment of Hagar. Lest we think of the merciful women as paragons of virtue, Sarai shows their shadow side. Her hospitality didn't include the slave girl, who bore Abram's son Ishmael when Sarai was infertile. Sarai banished Hagar and Ishmael twice to what seemed like inevitable death in the desert. Blithely passing on the same inhuman treatment she receives, she proves the dictum, "Hurt people hurt people."

They kept the angels busy, this Sarai-Abram duo. The angel, asking Hagar from whom she is escaping, gets a painfully direct reply: "I am running away from my mistress Sarai" (Gen. 16:8). Without God's gracious interventions, this pair could have done a lot more harm. In Sarai's story, as in many others, the first, best mercy is God's.

But to her credit, Sarai comes a long way and offers hope for change in a long life. Dramatizing her growth is her change of name, which occurs about the time most folks are joining AARP or collecting Social Security. The calligraphy of her new name here sparkles with stars in the A's.

Hostess to Angels

The new, improved Sarah does some short-order cooking in the heat of the day, which brings a huge reward. Abraham *offers* hospitality to strangers who turn out to be angels— guess who prepares the feast? (OK, he helps. But every woman who's ever entertained guests on short notice knows the sagging doubt that Sarah must have felt and the urge to thwack the effusive spouse.)

Much travel over many years must have worn her down: she couldn't collect Frequent Flier miles, and luxurious B & B's were few and far between. Yet somehow through all the traipsing around that probably seemed aimless, Sarah caught a glimpse of Abraham's vision. She learned to shelter his wild dreams—that vast image of countless stars and grains of sand must have resonated in her own longing for children. What a pact they must have made: as long as he held fast to the promise, she would help keep the dream alive.

Grandma to Nations

Like ourselves, Sarah is stupefied when she actually gets what she prayed for. Not only does God promise her a son, but a blessing that would cascade into "kings of people" (Gen. 17:16). "She will give rise to nations" must be the ultimate hospitality, but it all begins in laughter. Tucked behind the tent flap, she can't suppress her giggles at a couple of old fogeys conceiving a son.

She probably continues to laugh as she shelters a tiny person folded in her womb—there are a *lot* of laugh lines on that face. What a cosmic joke on all the doomsayers and negative voices who chorus, "You're too old for anything new, for potential, for starting a project." Hands folded tight across her swelling stomach, Sarah has the last laugh. An echo of her mirth would float from Nazareth many years later as her great-great-grandchild was announced in similarly bizarre circumstances: "Nothing is impossible for God."

As Sarah is portrayed here, we know that her wrinkly skin has comforted countless grandchildren. Her round contours defy diets, but provide a comfy lap for storytelling. Her hearty belly-laughter scatters stars in the blue of her ample skirts. She named her baby Laughter (Isaac in Hebrew) and probably taught him to count using the stars instead of an abacus. Her eyes look up with a trust that is only gradually learned. Model of a redeemed woman, she was great-great-grandmother of the Redeemer. No wonder Jesus turned out so well. Maybe he learned from her how to shelter the folks who couldn't find walls or roofs anywhere else.

Mary Magdalene

Merciful Transformation

Bear wrongs patiently

What are the traditional artistic representations of Mary Magdalene? In many portraits, she's weeping, penitent, half-naked, with disheveled hair. While the men around her stand, she lies prone.

To understand fully what's wrong with this stereotype, contrast it to Brother Mickey's art. Upright and clear, Mary points to a butterfly, the symbol of resurrected life. The verse on her scroll is central to her identity (and that of all Christians): "I have seen the Lord." She stands in a garden as witness to the core belief of Christianity: the resurrection.

This portrait shows the full person she was intended to be: independent woman, Jesus' beloved friend, apostle to the apostles commissioned by Jesus to tell extraordinary news, leader in the early church. In her, God's presence blooms as it did for any male disciple. The shift in the art suggests dramatic changes throughout the saga of Mary Magdalene.

Jane Schaberg summarizes the process: "No other biblical figure . . . has had such a vivid and bizarre postbiblical life in the human imagination, in legend and in art."[1] We may think *we're* noble when we "bear wrongs patiently"— the criticism, rejection, misunderstanding, or even firing. But Mary Magdalene has endured centuries of mud-slinging, her original role distorted. "Authorized by the risen Christ, she strangely has no authority."[2]

Nothing in scripture indicates that Mary Magdalene was a prostitute. Yet a hierarchy fearful of strong women perpetuated that myth until changes in the Roman calendar of 1969 and deletions from the Roman breviary of 1978. Since it takes a long time for scholarship to reach the public, some people even today still brand her with that stigma. Given the controversy surrounding her, it's a miracle her memory survived at all. That it did may be a tribute to the women who insisted on Mary Magdalene's integrity—or to the tenacity of grace.

A benign interpretation of what happened is "confusion." The problems stem from the conflation of several biblical texts: Luke 8:2, which says that Mary Magdalene had seven demons; Luke 7:37-39, which downgrades the anointing woman in Mark 14:3 from prophet to sinner, implying prostitution; and John 12:3, which makes Mary of Bethany the woman who anointed Jesus.

Pope Gregory the Great in the seventh century promulgated and lent authority to this conflation of texts about Mary Magdalene, the sinner of Luke 7, and Mary of Bethany. When the pope declared these three to be one person, he undermined her authority with the "counterweight of her sinfulness."[3] A sixteenth-century scholar who bravely suggested a correction to the prevailing theory was excommunicated.

The wrongs against Mary Magdalene fall into several categories:

- labeling her a former demoniac
- confining her to a role of financial support during the ministry
- ignoring her

- making her a prostitute
- replacing her leadership role with Peter's.

Crazy Woman

If, as Luke 8:2 suggests, she had seven demons, later generations might interpret that as mental illness or epilepsy. The New Testament never associates demonic possession with sin—and no *man*'s devils were assumed to be sexual. However, early commentators linked Mary Magdalene's condition with the seven deadly sins.[4] Over time, she became the sinful "madwoman—angry mad—in Christianity's attic."[5] One scholar comments on the irony, "It is hard to see how being tagged with the reputation of sevenfold demon-possession would not seriously undermine one's credibility as an apostle."[6] But what one generation read as madness, ours may see as resistance to the status quo, a protest against patriarchy and a kind of sanity.[7]

Financier

In Luke's Gospel, Mary Magdalene is one of several financially independent women who support Jesus' ministry. She is the only female disciple identified by her place of birth rather than her relationship to husband or son. Her title implies some prominence in her city, a commercial fishing center. The name Magdala in Hebrew means "tower," or "elevated, magnificent." While all of these are positives, the problem lies in reducing Mary Magdalene to *only* the role of financier.

Prophet Ignored

When Mark's Gospel uses the word "follower" to describe the women disciples, it implies full participation in belief and in preaching. Jesus welcomed them, never treated their contribution as inferior to the men's, and rejected any stereotyping or scapegoating of women.[8] Three Gospels mention Mary Magdalene at the foot of the cross. When others flee, she stays with the dying, wrongfully accused victim and arrives early at his tomb to anoint him. All four Gospels agree that she was one of the first witnesses to the resurrection.

Yet the early fathers of the church shifted the focus from Mary Magdalene to the other apostles, partially erasing her memory and soft-pedaling her intended role. Why? Partial answers include sexism, misogyny, opposition to women's leadership, and a growing emphasis on celibacy. If her character could be dismissed as romantic, crazed, or emotional, then her influence could be written off as insignificant. Jesus' efforts to overturn conventional values were minimized; rabbinical prejudices against women have persisted into our day.

Prostitute

Jesus rejected the idea of women as temptresses and redirected the blame for adultery to the lust in a man's heart (Matt. 5:28). In contrast, the emphasis on Mary Magdalene's sin almost obliterated her role as woman prophet. Focusing on her sexuality silenced her voice and removed her leadership. Put bluntly, "Mary Magdalen, chief female disciple, first apostle and beloved friend of Christ, would become transformed into a penitent whore."[9] For fourteen hundred years, the process reduced the power and authority of a major woman witness. Sadly, an exceptional woman today risks the same dangers: if she contributes her talents to the public sphere, critics may question her sanity or sexuality.

Peter's Rival

Without going too much into detailed scholarship, it's safe to say that the greater the role of Peter in a text, the more diminished the role of Mary Magdalene and other women leaders. The ancient traditions of the empty tomb and the appearances to the women in Matthew 28:1 and John 20:2 threatened some men because they suggest that Mary Magdalene can be considered a founder of Christianity. Such a significant role for her disrupts the idea, prevailing then and in some places now, that being male is the norm for being human. One unresolved puzzle is the fact that she disappears after John 20 and is never named in the company of the other disciples. Paul doesn't mention the women at all in his list of resurrection witnesses (1 Cor. 15).

Perhaps by balancing the roles of Mary, Peter, and the beloved disciple, John's community was trying to show a sharing of authority. Only when their three pieces of evidence are combined is the witness complete.[10] What kind of leadership would Mary Magdalene have exercised? We can only speculate. It *is* interesting that she calls Jesus *Rabbouni,* a diminutive form of endearment: "my dear or my little rabbi." This name undercuts mastery, deemphasizing Jesus as judge or ruler. His God is father to "all the brothers and sisters."[11]

A Transformed Order

The amount of energy that has gone into suppressing Mary Magdalene's voice is indicative that she must have posed a huge threat to the religious establishment.[12] Yet now that her true identity is being reclaimed, the butterfly here represents her transformation as well as Jesus' resurrection. She convinces the first disciples and skeptics throughout history that "love is stronger than death." What does she have to say to people today? Why does she stand here among the merciful women?

One of the best answers comes from Elizabeth Schüssler Fiorenza. She argues that the women's post-resurrection testimony contains a demand: "that one who hears it goes on to Galilee to continue the work of economic and social justice, for the poor, ill, oppressed, women, slaves." Liberating the exploited was an imperative for Mary, Jesus' mother, Mary Magdalene, and all the merciful women who followed. The resurrection vision imagines a renewed world free of suffering and death. Arguments over authority simply distract from that hope.

The most recent, popular portrayals of Mary Magdalene reduce her to a romantic relationship with Jesus. It is clear that the two loved each other, and she wears here the traditional red of fiery love. But we must be cautious about another form of restriction. This one places her in a personal, privatized role, when she can be much more.

Jesus calling Mary's name in the garden is a pivotal turning point, not only for her but for all subsequent human history. Her name is the hinge to a new order. It represents all tenderness and at the same time a surge of power so vast that all our metaphors shrink before it. If Jesus could come back from death, he could defeat any obstacle to being with those he loves. Washed in God's astounding compassion, Mary Magdalene is the first to realize that God can vanquish even death. Experiencing that mercy is the essential step to bearing wrongs patiently.

Veronica

Legendary Mercy

Comfort the sorrowful

Shakespeare imaged mercy as a gentle rainfall; here mercy is drawn in the compassionate curve of a woman's shoulder. We so often see Veronica in front of Jesus, wiping his face, that it is striking to see her in a different posture, holding her veil behind him. She touches the image so tenderly, bends over Christ so lovingly, that we respond: "Ah, so that's how mercy looks."

In contrast to the other historical or biblical characters, Veronica is a mythic figure. But sometimes we need legend more than bread. For centuries, wounded people have longed for the sweet relief of a touch like hers on their faces. Throughout humanity's violent history she holds up truth: "Everyone isn't as demented as the torturers." When the skin is aflame with pain, mercy falls soft and refreshing as mist.

A Costly Intervention

Few people appreciate what Veronica's courageous action must have cost. For a woman in her society to emerge alone from the crowd *and* to shed her veil broke all the cultural taboos. After the crucifixion, the author of Acts would link the quality of boldness with the companions of Jesus (4:13). For centuries afterward, women entered arenas where they were unwelcome or unprecedented, to bring the works of mercy.

Veronica is the patron saint of all who say, "Enough! I will do what I can to soothe this suffering." She doesn't stop the cruelty. She slows the death march for only minutes. But she tries. And her cameo appearance with Jesus encourages all who intervene when others trudge the tragic way of the cross. Helen Keller describes their efforts: although the world is full of suffering, it is full also of the overcoming of it.

God's Merciful Face

Veronica and those who follow her show us God's merciful face in human form. For Jesus, she was one of the few bright moments of relief in a dismal tunnel. Few people wept for him as she does. As he once wept for Lazarus.

God would later send this mercy to Elizabeth Ann Seton, quarantined in the Italian Lazaretto with her dying husband. Her journal records: "Found heavenly consolation, forgot prisons, bolts, and sorrows . . . became far more happy than I had been wretched." God's mercy would come again through prisoners in Nazi concentration camps who volunteered to nurse the victims of typhoid, an almost certain death sentence.

Veronica's compassionate posture and the black-violet cascade of her hair recall a key word in the Hebrew-Christian scriptures: overshadow. It was a figurative way to refer to God's protective presence. The cloud that accompanies Moses and the people overshadows them, directing them toward freedom (Ex. 40:34). In the story of the annunciation, the Spirit overshadows Mary, bringing a message that she should trust God to remain with her. Similarly, without a word, Veronica's gesture tells Jesus that he will pass through a horrific ordeal and emerge on the other side to peace.

Jesus on the Receiving End

Veronica is the only one in this company of merciful women whom Jesus identifies with more as the receiver than as the giver of mercy. From the deep well of pain, he acknowledges her effort and leaves his mark on her veil. That image then blesses all who *receive* the compassionate touch, the food, the therapy, the job, the attention, the medicine. It reminds us that at some times, we won't be the gracious giver. Even if we're sunk in misery, embarrassed to be stuck on the receiving end, Jesus is right there with us.

Giving mercy may make us feel strong and superior; receiving it balances the ego. The gift of mercy helps us understand that we can never earn God's utter graciousness. The message about mercy inscribed on Veronica's veil echoes Shakespeare:

It is twice blessed.

Blessing [her] who gives

and Him who receives.

CATERINE of SIENA

Catherine of Siena

A Mystic with Muddy Feet

Bury the dead

I envy her spunk. My friends and I were educated in a school like the Merion Mercy Academy of the early sixties. We were trained to be polite, passive, don't-rock-the-boat women who would *never question authority*. As a huge concession, "perkiness" might be tolerated, if it didn't interfere with the Way Things Were. The status quo was permanently engraved on stone pillars that didn't budge. Our role? Acquiesce, study, and become "good mothers and wives."

Anyone with that kind of background has to admire Catherine of Siena. For many years she was smack in the midst of Siena's warring factions. My Italian friends are the first to admit that Italian feuds are waged with a vehemence, drama, body language, verbal pyrotechnics, and linguistic finesse that we of milder cultures can only admire. Imagine, for instance, a traffic altercation in Rome during the heat of rush hour. As both parties roll up their sleeves, picture a woman stepping in.

At first the gathering crowd thinks she's crazy, but it soon develops that she is stubborn, blunt, outspoken—and she doesn't give an inch. Now up the ante. Imagine this same feisty upstart intervening in the armed, fourteenth-century conflict between Florence and the Avignon-based papacy. Nothing deters her. Passionately advocating justice, she sweetly informs the pope who has moved away from Rome that his court stinks of sin. (Gleefully, I picture the Reverend Mother of my high school cringing.) Perhaps she should come packaged with a warning: stand back. This woman kindles bonfires. And by the way, she's a doctor of the church.

She gives new meaning to the title "doctor." A misfit in the ivory tower, she's a mystic with muddy feet. Catherine holds a shovel because when plague swept through Italy, she had the courage to bury the dead. She shows how much one person can accomplish through prayer, letters, and the book in her hands, *The Dialogue.*

Antipasto/Appetizers

It's tempting to muse about apples not falling far from trees. Her passionate Mama Lapa screamed so loud, it frightened passersby on the Via dei Tintori. The family alone would have made a party—Catherine was the twenty-fourth child. Like most Italian families, hers lived to pour the wine and pass the pasta. As if that crew weren't enough, Catherine added a whole raft of friends and neighbors, an extended family so wide and devoted they called her "Mama." That merry company dining together gives a glimpse of heaven, which Catherine believed starts here and now.

Unsurprisingly, Catherine disliked the usual arrangements for religious women of her day. She refused a cell of wood or stone, launching into streets and prisons. There she found enough poor, miserable people and political problems to keep her plenty busy. After a lengthy argument with her family, her father finally conceded that Christ would not make a bad son-in-law. She then took on the habit of a Dominican tertiary, which has given the Dominicans bragging rights ever since.

A Hearty Love

Catherine's shovel is an important symbol not only for burial but also for building. Practically, she got her hands dirty. Understanding her perfectly, God speaks to her with a construction metaphor:

> It was necessary for me to build a bridge
>
> that would join your humanity
>
> with my divinity.

Wisely, God does not leave Catherine passive, but invites her participation in the divine enterprise:

> In order for you to have life,
>
> it is not enough
>
> that I have built this bridge,
>
> You must walk across it.

And walk she did—fearlessly, into all the hostile places of her world—as one writer calls her, "God's little tough."[1] She warmed up by settling feuds in Siena, then resolved the schism that had split the church for sixty-eight years. Like everything else in Catherine's experience, a bridge was a community affair, bulging with shops, taverns, and noisy crowds. None of it fazed her. As one biographer comments, "She may have been told that women were inferior, but she obviously did not believe it."[2]

No one intimidated her: neither popes nor prisoners. Calling Pope Gregory XI by the term of endearment "Sweet Babu," she convinced him to return to Rome from Avignon, ending a scandalous schism. He whined that she addressed him with an "intolerably dictatorial tone, a little sweetened." Maybe he should have been flattered. "Catherine never beat around the bush, even in conversations with God."[3]

Catherine liked the expression "hearty love," as one would describe a hearty breakfast or stew. Cooking skills formed her favorite metaphors. Through the incarnation of Christ, divinity and humanity were kneaded together, which must have made a fragrant, tasty loaf. To convince Pope Urban VI, Gregory's successor, to act with more sweetness and less bitterness, she prepared a candied orange, which she sent him with the recipe.

Against all the war, cruelty, disease, deception, violence, and horror of the fourteenth century, Catherine held fast to the vivid belief that God is madly in love with us, hungry for humanity. God's crazy obsession extended even to political prisoner Niccolo di Toldo, whom she counseled. At his execution, Catherine saw him welcomed into infinite mercy.

Lest we think that it's easy for a saint, Catherine endured vicious criticism for breaking the taboos that governed women in medieval society. For her to travel, to engage in public action, and to spend time with men—all would have been forbidden. In her *Dialogue*, she admits, "My life has been spent wholly in darkness." Even on her deathbed she questioned her motives and was plagued with self-doubts.

What Made Her Tick?

Contemporary women's studies have carefully observed how women gradually find their voice. Catherine's voice emerged from what she saw in the streets, which then drove her to contemplation in her room. Prayer then pushed her back into the quarrelsome arena of church and state politics, where she said boldly, "Stop it." To schism in the church, corruption in the clergy, wars of the city-states, political persecutions, gossip destroying relationships, Catherine said powerfully, "This cannot go on."[4]

She warns against the "tidiness" of a spiritual life governed by devotions and pieties, making us feel rather proud of ourselves. Instead she points us to the messiness of peoples' situations. The care she gave others sprang from the Christ whom she saw warmly as "bath and medicine, food and clothing, and a bed in which we can rest."

We see in Catherine's life what could happen in ours—if we really trusted God's promises, if we let God's fire fill us, if we weren't so neurotically afraid. She did a remarkable amount in a short time because she was only thirty-three when she died. Her brief but intense experience made her fluent in mercy: "On earth [mercy] is the language with which God speaks to us." How do we, in turn, learn the lingo? Bearing in mind God's mercy, we will not be mean-spirited with ourselves or others. God gives people abundant time, withholding nothing, blessing them with all creation.

The saints know "the truth of who they are because they have encountered the truth of who God is."[5] Catherine addressed God as "unutterable mercy." She once asked God, "Why did you so dignify us? With unimaginable love you looked upon your creatures within your very self, and you fell in love with us." God's words to her should reassure us:

> You are never alone.
> You have me.

Knowing *that,* how can we *not* show mercy?

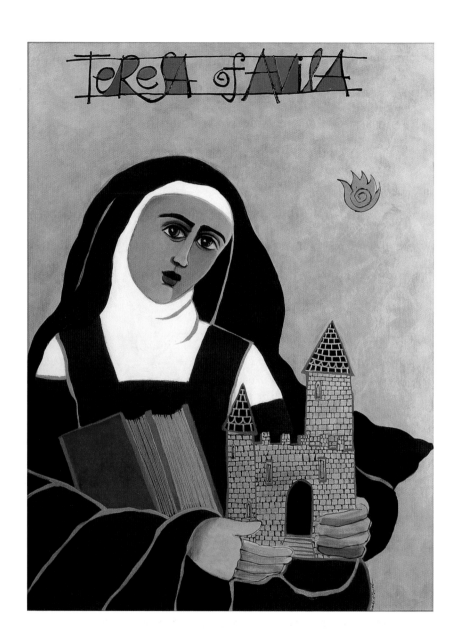

*T*eresa of Avila

Mercy Fest

Admonish the sinner

I sit on the deck of a Colorado ski resort, waiting for a friend to finish her last run. Beside me rest high-tech skis; I wear waterproof bibs and a down jacket. Soon we'll drive home on a six-lane interstate in a Toyota Corolla equipped with a CD player. Teresa of Avila would recognize almost nothing in that description, but as I wait I read her book. She becomes my companion in a world she never knew.

What draws me, a U.S. citizen of the twenty-first century, with four children, a career, a membership at the local gym, and a state-of-the-art computer, to a sixteenth-century

Spanish nun? In many ways, we are distant. Yet in all the ways that matter, we are close.

Advocate—and Charming Admonisher

Her work of mercy is to "admonish the sinner," but it is hard to imagine her "admonishing" except with wit. Consider the wry humor of her rhetorical question about the presence of God: "Do you think it's some small matter to have a friend like this at your side?" Speaking of God's generosity, she asks brusquely, one eyebrow arched, "Well, is it such a big thing that from time to time you turn your eyes to look upon one who gives you so much?"

"Admonishing" sounds gentle in contrast to the Inquisition of Teresa's day. Its forces attempted to change people through threats and violence. One suspects that Teresa's humor had longer-lasting effects.

Perhaps Teresa could admonish others successfully because she was hard on herself. She often strikes a note of self-deprecation: "If I had understood as I do now that in this little palace of my soul dwelt so great a King, I would not have left him alone so often." She is filled with regret for squandering her early years on empty conversations and foolish pursuits.

She encourages us because she wavered too: "One day I am so full of courage that I would do anything for God. The next day I would not kill an ant if I met the slightest opposition." Admonishing herself, she insisted that her work be faithful to the gospel. This meant demeaning scrutiny and heartless revision.

Thus she could admonish not just one sinner but a whole sinful system, reforming not only the Carmelite order but also attitudes about women and approaches to prayer. A sucker for affection, she admitted easily, "I could be bought for a herring." Passionate, brisk, practical, energetic, and fun, she perfectly mentors the young, and indeed all contemporary women.

Teresa was a passionate advocate for young women. They shouldn't have to endure what she did as a novice: too many women jammed into one house making trivial conversation (Tupperware party, anyone?). Instead, she believed they should have gracious, orderly spaces where they could turn inward. In an era when women could easily have spent their youth, time, and energy on the drudgery of repeated tasks, she called them to contemplation, echoing Jesus' rebuke to Martha and welcome to Mary. She encourages anyone who doubts that rich potential: "My daughters, we are not hollow inside."

To fully appreciate Teresa's empowering of women, contrast her attitude with the prevailing wisdom. One blessedly forgotten Francisco de Osuna writes: "Since you see your wife going about visiting many churches, practicing many devotions and pretending to be a saint, lock the door; and if that isn't sufficient, break her leg. . . . It is enough for a woman to hear a sermon and then put it into practice. If she desires more, let a book be read to her while she spins, seated at her husband's side."[1] Imagine how Teresa might respond: a hearty snort.

An early advocate of equal rights, she speaks the language of the twenty-first century when she tells her sisters: "They say that for a woman to be a good wife toward her husband she must be sad when he is sad, and joyful when he is joyful, even though she may not be so. (See what subjection you have been freed from, Sisters!)" But she's an equal-opportunity critic of both vocations: "May God preserve us from stupid nuns!"

The novelist Toni Morrison might have been echoing Teresa when she said, "We are all traditionally rather proud of ourselves for having slipped creative work in there between the domestic chores and obligations. I'm not sure we deserve such big A pluses for that."[2]

The Books

It is ironic that Teresa carries a book. As a woman in sixteenth-century Spain, she was forbidden to preach or even comment on scripture. Yet her authoritative voice boomed larger than institutional constraints. Silenced, she found a way to speak: through books, letters, spiritual direction—all qualified by sweet deferrals to authority, coy disclaimers that she had no idea what she was talking about.

Teresa's books shifted dramatically away from common practices of prayer—rote formulas addressed to a distant God. Those who practiced mental prayer or contemplation in her day were few and marginal. Most people considered direct experience of God, without the intervention of clergy, subversive.

When contemporary spiritual writers were discouraging "corporeal images" as an obstacle to prayer, Teresa delighted in them. She gave Christians images close to the daily life of their time: the interior castle, the watered garden, the beehive, the heart of God like the innermost, edible core of the palmetto, the argument set up like a chessboard.[3]

Indeed, she performed a great mercy to those who have difficulty wrapping their minds around (mostly male) abstractions. In her day, spirituality was the preserve of educated men, rigidly defended by thuggish Inquisitors. Her concrete images, earthy as the brown habit she wears, do a great service for seekers of all centuries. She reminds those who "have no learning" that they have something infinitely precious inside. Given such richness, her daughters shouldn't care about the favor of the bishop.

One mercy is the practicality of Teresa's deeply feminine metaphors: for instance, comparing prayer to the stages of watering a garden, with God's grace the culminating gift of rain. "Recollection of the senses" seems like an arid concept until Teresa explains it in terms of bees entering a beehive to make honey. So the senses are drawn inward to concentrate on God. But nothing is forced: once lassoed, the senses can wander freely, like bees swarming in and out of the hive.

Underlying all the images is perhaps the greatest mercy:

accessibility to a God who gives the soul all it desires. The face of God that Teresa reveals is not punitive or distant, but precious as a lover, close as a friend.

Castles Metaphoric and Actual

In addition to her book, Teresa holds a castle. It may look here like a frail sugar-cube construction, but she built both books and convents sturdy, to survive formidable opposition. Her sublime reflection on prayer, *The Interior Castle*, is based on an image of the soul as a crystal castle. She expands eloquently on the biblical theme of many rooms in the Father's house (John 14:2). Although *The Interior Castle* was written under pressure in a short time, an eyewitness describes Teresa during the process: when "she was writing she was in prayer."

Indeed, the gate to the castle is prayer. The reader then moves through seven chambers representing stages on the journey to God. In the center, God dwells in splendor, illuminating the whole castle. There God joins the soul to God's self in what she terms a "marriage." Despite the need to pay attention to other affairs, the "soul never moved from that room." We might prefer a more organic image now; the castle may be tied to excessive wealth. But when most households were dark and dreary, this transparent dwelling that lets in abundant light must have had wide appeal.

While most of her contemporaries preached that the primary form of prayer should be vocal and by rote, Teresa challenged people: How could they mouth words without reflecting? How could they address God's majesty as thoughtlessly as they would speak to a slave?

In an atmosphere dominated by the Inquisition's obsession with religious purity, she pleaded for "holy freedom" on behalf of her daughters. She danced lightly around those who would censor her, maintaining an agile step while trumpeting her inadequacies. How could others condemn her when she beat them to it? As she claims she's a wretched woman, incapable of doing anything for God, readers suspect a wise, self-protective grin whispering behind the words.

Teresa keeps the Inquisition hounds at bay by throwing them bones: referring to herself as a trained parrot with "womanly dullness of mind." She camouflages her identity by pretending to report the experiences of *others*. She compares herself and her readers to people with "souls and minds so scattered they are like wild horses." One can imagine her gullible censors nodding approvingly: at least one woman knows her place!

Her legacy is even more than the written word. Teresa believed firmly that love flowed into work. Like Teresa of Calcutta, she thought it a privilege "to work in the garden of so great a Lord." She spent years on the road enduring wretched travel conditions to assure safe and sacred spaces for others. The seventeen convents she founded were distant from each other, and road conditions were abominable. Thus her description of traveling securely to God has a special immediacy: "Whoever truly loves you, my God, travels by a broad and a royal road." While she couldn't have envisioned interstate highways or jet travel, she knew the source of all security:

> Hardly do we stumble . . .
> when you, O Lord, give us your hand.

The Arrow

With characteristic aplomb, Teresa describes God touching her with a flaming arrow. This is how Bernini depicts her in his famous seventeenth-century sculpture. She speaks of a long gold spear piercing her entrails, leaving her on fire with love of God.

The arrow flies both ways: God also delights in finding us. Teresa reports a conversation with God in which God asks, "Who are you?" She replies, "I am Teresa of Jesus. And who are you?" God answers, "I am Jesus—of Teresa."

The rich interior castle was for her, a woman who might have originally seemed too shallow and flighty for it, the defining proof of God's mercy. She might thus serve as patron saint for all who get the mercy of a second chance. Unlike Catherine of Siena, who accomplished a great deal before her death at age thirty-three, Teresa encourages those who start slow. Mentor to the middle-aged as well as to the young, she was forty-seven when she began her great work of reform. She warmed up gradually, but for the last twenty years of her life, she was a dynamo.

Perhaps her energy surged from her deeply rooted identity. We share her gusto when we accomplish a project, nurture a friendship, earn a paycheck or an award, raise a healthy child, climb a mountain, or run a race. Through us floods some mysterious, high-octane fuel that Teresa would name divine energy.

Convinced that God was by her side, the spouse of her soul and her best friend, she could do anything. We too can summon that presence, believing in Teresa's words:

> However long we live,
> we could never wish
> for a better friend than God.

The Blowing Veil

When the abundant joy of the Communion of Saints is coursing through your veins, it's hard to stand still. You gotta dance. So Teresa's veil is blowing to suggest a wild tarantella, tambourines, a loud mariachi band, nothing sedate or stodgy. She encouraged her daughters to dance like David before the ark.

She led the sisters in rituals like this one, which anyone can appreciate who's ever come home from camp with lice. Imagine the itchy annoyance of the pests infesting rough clothing in Spain's heat. Then imagine Teresa leading the procession, blessing people, rooms, and beds, singing, "Do Thou keep all nasty creatures out of this serge!"[4] As in all lives of the saints, the pesky critters predictably vamoosed. One more facet of mercy's infinite faces . . .

Thérèse of Lisieux

Little Mercies

Visit the imprisoned

How do we read her, this enormously popular saint who raises questions for contemporaries? She finds flowers under every step; we walk on asphalt. She advocates the way of the child; we struggle toward adult maturity. She is cloaked in nineteenth-century piety; we like our prose lean and unsentimental. She comes from an impossibly loving family; we confront the daily soap operas of dysfunctional ones.

And yet . . .

Dorothy Day, sentenced to thirty days in jail for protesting the 1957 civil-defense drill in New York City, meditates on her favorite saint. This woman is the subject of her new book: Thérèse of Lisieux. Day saw prison as the ideal setting for Thérèse's Little Way. There, each illness, ugliness, infirmity, indiginity, search, idleness, noise, and rule could bring one closer to God. "Every event seems calculated to intimidate," Day wrote. Because prison was the site of "thwarted human freedom," she turned to Thérèse to celebrate the ordinary. Just as the tiny atom had wrought havoc, so the Little Way had explosive, transformative power.[1]

This modern link was not Thérèse's only connection to jail. Nothing could seem more remote from an isolated Carmelite cloister than the harsh penal system. And yet . . .

Sheltered throughout her life by devoted parents and loving sisters, Thérèse "adopted" a murderer. The notorious Pranzini, who had killed a woman, her maid, and her child, refused a priest before his execution. Feeling his estrangement from humanity, Thérèse imaginatively entered the prison, understood his thirst, prayed for him, and felt responsible for a last-minute hint of repentance.[2]

Perhaps Thérèse liberates from many kinds of enforced confinement. She saw enormous potential in the daily grind. Both Gerald May, author of *Man's Search for Meaning,* and the

Italian psychiatrist Roberto Assagioli knew that sometimes the only choice left is how we react to a situation. Jailed by the fascists in 1939 for his antiwar stance, Assagioli claimed his "essential freedom and power."[3] He turned a prison sentence that could have prompted anger, rebellion, or self-pity into an opportunity for growth and a spiritual retreat.

So, despite dreams of being a missionary in Vietnam, Thérèse responded with gusto to confined circumstances. Shaped by her own reading, she shed the syrupy piety of her older sisters. She chose selectively from the tradition and created afresh. At thirteen, she decided to be not slave to but mistress of her acts, and she abandoned her weepy scruples.

Tender Mercies

Thérèse's story begins with the spirituality of her parents. To us, it might seem treacly, but their belief gave their daughters the foundation for faith. Her childhood was "inundated with joy," she writes in *The Story of a Soul*. Her parents encouraged her fondness for grass, flowers, and fishing. The whole family indulged her as "the little queen," the perennial baby, their favorite with carefully curled blonde hair. When she spent a couple nights at her school (within walking distance of home), the family visited with pastries.

If that all sounds over the top, stay tuned. The harsh facts speak volumes: Thérèse's mother died when she was four. She records immeasurable sadness in her autobiography. Her sister Celine, given a beautiful apricot, saves it for a mother too sick to eat it. Later, five little girls line up beside the bed for their mother's final anointing, and Thérèse is told to kiss her mother for the last time.

Then when Thérèse was nine, her beloved Pauline, a "second mother," left home to join the Carmelite convent. Crying "Pauline is lost to me!" Thérèse felt the departure like a sword to her heart. This loss led to her own sickness and constant headaches. She describes the people seated around her bed "like a row of onions, looking at me as though I were a strange beast." Her ungilded personality shines through in a few genuine phrases like this and "my spelling, which was nothing less than original."

In the same year Thérèse entered Carmel (at fifteen) her father began to have "mental trouble," which is glossed over in some biographies. Phrases like "three years in a mental hospital" and "serious relapse" are tucked quietly into the chronology. But the tragedy deeply affected a sensitive teenager who loved her father dearly. She wasn't allowed to visit, and gossips blamed his mental collapse on her leaving home. As she matured, Thérèse revised her glorious concepts of martyrdom. She came to see the martyr as her gentle father, lying in a 500-bed mental hospital with a handkerchief covering his head.[4]

Yet despite these ordeals, Thérèse drew on early experiences of mercy with her parents and sisters. She recalls their tenderness: "I was really a child who was fondled and cared for like few other children on earth, especially among those deprived of their mothers."

Riddled with Pinpricks

In her photo which inspired Brother Mickey's art, taken at age fifteen, she is bright, plucky—and trying to look older by wearing her hair "up." This spunky teen is not set in the angelic mold later admirers would force on her. Because of some doubt among local authorities that she could enter Carmel so young, she took her cause to the pope! Almost as if foreseeing her death at age twenty-four, she insisted she belonged in the convent. In a lovely metaphor, her father shows her small white flowers, saying that God's care for them symbolized what Jesus had done for Thérèse.

Authentically human, Thérèse wasn't immune from irritation. Reading between the lines, we can only imagine how grumpy Sister St. Pierre annoyed the young girl. Describing the crochety nun, Thérèse admits, "I knew it was not easy to please" her. Thérèse's daily ritual was to carry Sister's little bench, hold her, get her from chapel to dining hall, "seat her skillfully," and turn back her sleeves in a certain way before eating—all to the tune of constant criticism.

Another nun behind her in the chapel made "clicking" noises at prayer. Given the close quarters and intensity of the community, it must have set Thérèse's teeth on edge. Add to the scene a prioress who was probably neurotic and the jealousy of some nuns toward the Martin sisters, and it seems a recipe for disaster.

And yet . . .

Thérèse seized every opportunity, imaging her good work as strewing flowers. When her perspective clouded, she wrote: "At close range . . . the roses disappear; one feels that to do good is as impossible without God's help as to make the sun shine at night." Having that strong identification with

Christ observed in many of the merciful women, she believed: "Thérèse had vanished as a drop of water is lost in the immensity of the ocean. Jesus alone remained."

While some see her path as saccharine in its gilded purity, the truth for Thérèse was expressed through metaphors such as a foggy country, clothing stained in blood, a table filled with bitterness, a dark tunnel, a thick, underground darkness. After receiving the Eucharist, when most people expect emotional consolation, she writes, "it is the time when I received the least." The harsh side of her last illness is clear: "Do not believe I am swimming in consolations; oh no, my consolation is to have none on earth."

"Everything Is Grace"

Despite this aridity, Thérèse had found treasure. From human mercy, she intuits divine mercy. "I knew that if I was loved on earth, I was also loved in heaven." Later she writes the line shown here in her journal: "My vocation is love." Marcus Aurelius once saw how the color of one's thought dyes one's soul. In Thérèse's case, the color of her love dyes her experience. Her outlook is completely colored by trusting surrender to a Great Love.

The attitude must have been difficult to maintain in an atmosphere where nuns judged each other and criticized innovation. Many saw the Carmelite way of life as penance deflecting God's anger. Mercifully, Thérèse saw herself as a little child, sleeping fearlessly in her father's arms, hiding her face in his hair.

Thérèse developed a distinctly feminine approach to spirituality. For years, people had equated holiness with grandiose male adventures: boldly fighting battles, founding organizations, dying as martyrs. The ordinary way she envisioned fit the individual nooks and crannies of unique lives. She shifted the emphasis away from heroic deeds, indeed from *any* accomplishment. Instead, she was conscious of "remaining little," the great God holding her.

Contemporary women may resist the idea that all their endeavors are small—and indeed they are not. But where Thérèse seems helpful is in an arena where most women are stuck anyway. Most of us *do* fold laundry, referee crayons, pack lunches, deal with irritating people, and unload the dishwasher. Her work of mercy was healing the sick and feeding the hungry in the convent. Wittily, she describes the nunny tyrant of the laundry as an old clock, needing frequent rewinding. Thérèse shows, as few spiritual leaders ever had, the grace in the ordinary task.

So too she frees those imprisoned by illness, who do not seem to be actively reforming the world. During her final illness, Thérèse felt as if "stretched out on iron spikes." The sisters around her bed spoke of visions and ecstasies; she herself knew nothing but pain. In addition to the ordeal of her lungs disintegrating and her slow suffocation, she endured mental agony. She imagined herself in a black hole, yet she clung to a favorite quotation from the seductive Song of Songs: "Draw me, we shall run after you in the odor of your ointments" (1:3).

The Joy of a Constellation

During Thérèse's last illness one sister said of her, "She is always making those who come to visit her laugh. There are times when one would pay to be near her. I believe she will die laughing, she is so happy." She had a whole repertoire of puns, tricks, and jokes about herself and her doctor's inability to help. In the hot infirmary, her sister Pauline tried to predict the date of her death. Thérèse was absorbed in *now,* indifferent to which feast she'd die on, and laughed, "eat 'dates' . . . I have been too much taken in by 'dates.'"

And yet . . . Thérèse told her sisters not to worry if they saw in her no sign of joy at the moment of death: "To die of love does not mean to die in transports." She also asked that no poisonous medicines be left within reach. Because of her superior's bizarre refusal of morphine, she suffered so intensely she feared she would take her own life.

In one of the ironies that seem to characterize her, Thérèse is quoted in the *Catechism of the Catholic Church*: "For me prayer is an aspiration of the heart, it is a simple glance directed to heaven, it is a cry of gratitude and love in the midst of trial as well as joy. . . ." Yet elsewhere she admits that she slept through her prayers for seven years running, a fact the *Catechism* does not mention.

She noted another irony: that one who wanted to die as a missionary or martyr would die in bed from tuberculosis, the most common disease in Europe. But justice would come in time: because of her longing to travel, Thérèse became patron saint of airline pilots.

The flowers that surround her can easily be sentimental-ized. But in her day, the symbol was fresh and natural, a relief from layers of piety accumulated over the centuries. The revolution Thérèse introduced to spiritual imagery parallels the innovations in poetic language made by her contemporaries William Butler Yeats and Gerard Manley Hopkins.

At that time, no one thought of women priests—except Thérèse. She was frustrated with mediocre sermons and the difficulty of finding a priest who understood her. Sounding contemporary, she advocated homilies with a solid base in scripture, not in the commonly used pious stories or imagined scenes. In 1897, she told her sister Celine that she would die at the time of the June ordinations, when, if she were male, she would have been ordained.

In Thérèse's life, holiness was a communal event. Just as the woman of the parable calls in her friends and neighbors, so too Thérèse's writings began as storytelling for her sisters. Carol Flinders explains, "[women] see the incandescent superstar for what it is, but they see the constellation in which it has come into being, too, the reverent and loving care that has surrounded and nourished it. They see how much we have to do with one another, how profoundly we require one another."[5] Mercifully, we are given to each other.

CATHERINE MCAULEY

"Let us fit young women for earth without unfitting them for heaven"

Catherine McAuley

An Affectionate Alliance

Counsel the doubtful

I watched in awe as the portraits emerged—from a charcoal sketch against a dull background to glowing gold, textured plaid, warm skin tones. From stick figures to full-blown women, they evolved through the artist's genius. Brother Mickey intuits exactly where to place a violet highlight or a black outline. Here he tucks wit; there, inspiration. A few brush strokes transform.

So it goes when mercy flowers, spontaneous as art. The seeds may come from another's example, a driving need, a

Bible passage. Then the abstract quality blooms: here in the Sudan, there in Philadelphia. From the basic outline given by tradition, it takes on color and vibrancy in individual lives. Deanne DeCrescenzo, a graduate of Merion Mercy, writes of its emergence in a young woman: "It is clear to me now that what has most shaped my character is my education and understanding of mercy. I have been instructed in lessons of the heart." Deanne echoes Thomas Aquinas's definition of mercy: "a heart suffering over the sufferings of others." Catherine McAuley would have nodded proudly, sipping her tea.

Early Seeds

The Georgian doorways of eighteenth-century Dublin were not only beautiful in themselves. They symbolized the future opening to a girl who walked through them a century later. Descriptions of young Catherine McAuley agree on her brilliant coloring, blonde hair, attractive figure, and a poignant expression that could quickly turn into "real hearty fun."[1]

Her father, architect James McAuley, was an important influence before his death when Catherine was four. Even after she had forgotten his appearance and voice, she remembered his commitment to the poor. Her mother, Elinor, protested that their home was "cluttered with derelicts." But James kept the door open to the needy. He led what today we'd call a "house church," planting early seeds of mercy. Catherine's regular experience with the institutional church didn't come till she was in her mid-twenties. Only then did she attend liturgies with an ordained cleric; her essential character had been shaped long before.

Her mother's death not long after her father's may have explained another, sadder door. Catherine said the tomb was never closed to her. Those who knew her noticed an "elusive sadness" in her expression. It would be understandable: after her parents' deaths, she had different guardians, experiences of wealth and poverty, good care and neglect, loneliness and social life.

These losses and fluctuations were compounded by the slammed door of Protestant–Catholic relations in a decidedly unecumenical era. Her younger brother and sister were raised Protestant; Catherine held fast to Catholicism. Much of the energy in her early life seemed directed toward converting good people whom she loved. It would be anachronistic to contrast contemporary religious tolerance with her attitudes. But given intense hostilities in Ireland of that day, the remarkable thing was that Catherine got along so well with people of other traditions. Indeed, she learned about serving the poor from Quakers in the Callaghan household that "adopted" her.

As with several of the other merciful women, the early background seems a formula for disaster. Yet from the deaths, relocations, and changing guardians, what emerges is a clear path to later life. An inheritance from the Callaghan family gave Catherine the money to build the first House of Mercy on Baggott Street. Called "Kitty's folly" by her critics, its red doors eventually opened on September 24, 1827, the feast of Our Lady of Mercy.

Catherine appears to have been motivated partly by grief over a servant girl who had asked her for help. The plight of serving women has been dramatized in contemporary films: they were completely at the mercy of their employers, often receiving food and clothing but no pay. Victimized and voiceless, one girl appealed to Catherine. Although Catherine tried to get help from a Dublin organization, deadlines for applications were inflexible and in the intervening time, the girl disappeared. That memory may have prompted McAuley's maxim, "the poor need help today, not next week."

Again, what appeared to be failure led to new resolve. Theologian Catherine Hilkert explains the dynamic: For some people, negative experiences only confirm the belief that life is absurd. But those who can transcend them rely on prior experiences of meaning and joy. "It is precisely the life and love we have known, the compassion of God we have tasted, that prompts us to say that life could be different, that peace is possible, that relationships can be mended."[2]

Catherine saw women's needs for housing and education and studied how best to serve them. With a real sense of professionalism, she visited schools in Ireland, England, and France, studying classroom management, standards, and procedures.

In an alley McAuley discovered a little girl whose parents had died of fever. The girl literally had nowhere to go, and this aching need prompted Catherine to action. To her school and refuge for unemployed servants, she added an orphanage.

Open Doors

Catherine also opened doors for "the walking nuns," part of a nineteenth-century phenomenon that dramatically changed the cloistered tradition. Perhaps as a response to the Industrial Age, over six hundred communities of women applied to Rome for recognition to do active work *outside* the convent walls. They were oriented *first* toward mission, "rather than mission being an overflow of monastic life."[3]

When Catherine began the House of Mercy, she insisted that her group would not be vowed religious. She envisioned a group of volunteers loosely bound by common ideals. They would visit the sick poor in hospitals and at home, but not be bound by canonical regulations.

Resistance to such a novelty stemmed from the fact that people didn't know how to think of Catherine's group. Some clergy members encouraged tighter organization, and local gossips criticized the women's freedom to come and go. Catherine and her sisters felt no attraction to the convent, but gradually they modified their lifestyle, studied various rules, and trained with sisters at the Presentation Convent.

McAuley was repelled by some of what she saw there and was especially uncomfortable with distinctions between superior and "subjects." Perhaps the Quaker influence led her to resist hierarchy. She refused the title Reverend Mother and never touted herself as "the Foundress." As soon as she was professed with simple vows, she fled back to Baggot Street. Some even remember that in her urgency to return she skipped breakfast—which must have cranked up the gossip mills!

She founded the Sisters of Mercy as a compromise, not an end in itself but a means to spread the charism of mercy. The advantage of nuns with flexibility emerged clearly when a cholera epidemic hit Dublin in 1832. McAuley prioritized the care of victims, reassigning sisters from other ministries. Wisely caring for the caregivers, she sent the sisters out in teams of four, relieved every four hours. Knowing how hard her sisters worked, she encouraged them to relax and have fun. The cholera treatment they developed was so successful that one of the Mercy nurses used it again with Florence Nightingale in the Crimea.

Constant problems were the poor health of the sisters, their deaths at early ages, and the skepticism of some parish priests who treated them like children. One Reverend Kelly doubted that the "unlearned sex could do anything but mischief by trying to assist the clergy."[4] Meanwhile, McAuley worried constantly about meeting enormous demands on her resources.

Yet a lightness balanced her worries. She exchanged rhymed doggerel with her sisters and puzzled over the gift of a cow. At Tullamore the group lived in "rooms so small two cats could scarcely dance in them." Due to a misunderstanding over paying a bill, she once "hid out" from a lawman— which "caused more laughing than crying." One bishop called her "the greatest enemy the fashionable world has"— which didn't seem to bother her.

Within McAuley stirred the first steps toward ecumenism—calcified customs cracked; doors creaked open an inch. Knowing the intense Protestant–Catholic animosity in Ireland, it is startling to read of a bazaar that brought her work almost £300, contributed largely by Protestants. They shared her Christian ideals, and she had maintained her early family connections with their tradition.

Given centuries of English–Irish hostility, Catherine also made huge inroads on the status quo. Consider this odd combination: Before Princess Victoria became Queen of England, she decorated boxes for Catherine's bazaar. Daniel O'Connell, the Irish Liberator, carved the turkey for Christmas dinner at Baggot Street. Her English novices in Ireland and her own journey to found a house in England were dramatic reversals of the bloody history.

All Aboard!

Her travels were often excruciating; people seemed to plunk the nuns into damp, cold, prisonlike quarters. McAuley and her friends, marooned in miserable conditions, marveled at what local pastors considered "prepared" rooms. They laughed at the "Newfoundland Ice" of chilly Ireland and oatmeal that broke teeth. Catherine knew the dance steps of her day and encouraged her sisters to "dance every evening"—if only to keep warm! Extensive travel led McAuley to a complaint voiced by some jet setters today: "When I awake in the morning, I ask myself where I am."

The speed at which the small movement spread worldwide (opening doors in the United States, New Zealand, the Philippines, Newfoundland, and Latin America) shows how gladly people join positive work. At the time of McAuley's death, there were one hundred Sisters of Mercy; a hundred years later there were twenty-three thousand. Today, the extensive work of lay colleagues and associates returns to McAuley's original ideal—not necessarily vowed religious but autonomous laypeople.

Catherine delighted in the blessing of her colleagues: "Not one cold stiff soul appears from the day they enter . . . this is the true spirit of Mercy flowing on us." As she lay dying, her final gesture was to have prepared a "comfortable cup of tea" for the sisters with her.

Women friends today, sharing a cup of something steamy, relate to this hallmark gesture, as they would to the warm shawl of sisterhood. Catherine's sense of fun would glow now in e-mails. She might type her rhyme:

> Turn what you can into a jest
> And with few words dismiss the rest.

It's not hard to imagine one of her colleagues, anticipating her visit, reading McAuley's plans on a computer screen: "I am determined not to behave well and you must join me."

A Mighty Tenderness

The ivy-covered Limerick House of Mercy had ancient history and a tranquil, enclosed garden. In a sense its doors symbolized the two movements of McAuley's life. "The door in the wall [of the garden] opens on timelessness," she wrote. Her intense activity was centered in God, her "dear good old acquaintance." She focused on mercy, "the principal path pointed out by Jesus Christ." With characteristic humor, she wrote, "prayer will do more [to solve our problems] than all the money in the Bank of Ireland."

Yet the house also bordered a wretched slum. The needs there motivated Catherine to become nurse, teacher, administrator, fund-raiser, spiritual director, and writer. Between the two doors of contemplation and action, she would live out merciful service. She would begin a community which Leonard Cohen's song "Sisters of Mercy" later described:

If your life is a leaf that the seasons tear off and condemn
They will bind you with love that is graceful and green
    as a stem.

Elizabeth Ann Seton

Mercy Family Style

Instruct the ignorant

Carol is the single mom of five splendid children. They are the center of her life—it's obvious in every conversation or letter. In e-mails she worries about the safety of a son in the Marines or a daughter's gall bladder surgery. One child travels abroad; another chooses a college. Most of Carol's energy pours into her family; her career seems secondary. Knowing her is a window into the life of Elizabeth Ann Seton.

Although she is rightly praised as the founder of the American Catholic schools and the Sisters of Charity, that work seems to be an expansion of the family which engrossed her. Her life might be pictured by a series of widening circles.

The Nucleus

Elizabeth's mother died when she was three, and the lack of a mother figure when she was growing up seems central to understanding Elizabeth. Her stepmother was distant; Elizabeth's beloved father died when he brought medical aid to the victims of yellow fever. Between the ages of eight and nineteen, Elizabeth lived with different relatives, shifted from house to house. No wonder she was so thrilled to marry William Seton and have "my own home at twenty—the world."[1]

Because she had missed a mother's care, Elizabeth was intent on providing it for her children. She defined herself: "The only word I have to say to every question is: I AM A MOTHER." But when her husband's father died, the Setons moved out of their home to care for his young brothers and sisters. Seven more children needed a mom!

The Circle Expands

Seton's growth proves one mother's idea that the time of raising children is an internship in tenderness. There we learn "how to touch, how to feed, how to tend, how to heal, how to care, how to love." Through parenthood, we practice setting aside our own interests for the sake of others.

But it doesn't end when the children grow up. Instead, child rearing may be only the rehearsal, the warm-up exercise. "Having practiced our scales, played the daily exercises of love for our children . . . now we come to the concerto. Having loved our own, we now can love the world. Now we rise to the task for which our parenting prepared us."[2]

Seton came to that task inadvertently. Widowed at twenty-nine with five children and her husband's siblings to support, Seton could find few avenues where a woman could make a living. Ostracized from her wealthy family because of her conversion to Catholicism, she skimped on groceries and appealed to her friends.

Before Elizabeth gave mercy, she received it from these friends. They had known her in youth as the charming Betsey Bayley, the doctor's highly educated daughter who played Mozart on the piano beneath the candelabra. Seton herself commented, "They know not what to do with me. But God knows." To their credit, several friends remained loyal to that laughing girl when her family's needs must have become a royal pain. Harsher critics referred to the "poor deluded Mrs. Seton."

Her journal records various schemes to make a living. Some proposals were a tea store or a china shop, or—as a last resort—a small school. She took delight in finally moving away from relatives to her own home, where she earned three dollars a week for each boarder she took in. The modest income would make her and her family "less a burden" to friends. "The pleasure of doing something for my darlings makes every labor easy." Nevertheless, the protective mum worried about the boys' rude influence on her own children.

Seton found herself in the position of many single parents today: under enormous pressure simply to cope. Grieving for her husband, father, and close friends, she must have been terrified when her oldest daughter, Annina, grew ill. She cared for her with whatever minimal medicines and rudimentary nursing skills she had. But her daughter's death desolated Elizabeth, leaving her in depression for many months. She said of herself, "I was so often expecting to lose my senses. . . . I did not know much what I did."

When her daughter Rebecca was sick for five years, Seton wrote, "she is wrapped in the very nerves of my soul." If Elizabeth had been given to typical nineteenth-century pieties, she would have provided the girl with rosaries and scapulars. But she knew her "saucy" daughter too well for that. She asked her friend Julia Scott to send a doll and ribbons to brighten the sick room.

When Scott sent a ball gown, Elizabeth (by that time, a habit-clad nun) tried it on and pirouetted for her daughter's delight. Because Bec craved music, Seton "sang her old songs of thirty years ago." But Rebecca died at fourteen. Seton recorded the event without pious flummery. Her words are as stark as her black dress: "I have lost the little friend of my heart."

After so much tragedy, it would be understandable for a mother to retire from action and grieve. That route was denied Seton, because she had three more children to raise. She writes, "If I was not obliged to live in these dear ones, I should unconsciously die in [Rebecca]."

Yet she continued mothering. Her vivacious daughter Kit was much more interested in parties than in the convent scene. Seton apologized to her friends, "Kit's expenses push you a little hard," then asked for dancing, painting, and piano lessons.

Her thoughtless sons seemed to ruin every opportunity she arranged, squandering the money she worked so hard to send. To a few friends she admitted that her boys were "a thorn in the heart." Her journal is brutally honest about their lack of talent and irresponsibility. Yet somehow, the heart pierced and expanded by motherhood grew to embrace countless children.

The Schools

After all she had endured with her children, she could treat her work of education almost casually. A donor gave her land for a novitiate at Emmitsburg, Maryland, where she could educate "catholic female children." "I have the prospect of receiving many daughters," she wrote. The line seems poignant in light of Annina's and Rebecca's deaths. Yet Elizabeth was joyful about being able to assist the poor, visit the sick, comfort the sorrowful, and teach children. The self-deprecating disclaimer creeps in: initially, even good friends wouldn't trust her with children meant "to bear a part in polished society."

Remarkably, this woman without a college degree designed a system of education that was ordered and intelligent. Seton drew on her own reading and the ways she had taught her children. She joked that her authority as "the Old Lady" was a matter of "smiling and caressing," while the teachers had all the trouble. She seemed astonished when the school grew to fifty, then a hundred children. Her self-definition was always in maternal terms: "an old woman to whom the nearly one hundred souls in our house look for their daily solace of a mother's smile."

The growing numbers of sisters and students necessitated a structure for her group, the Sisters of Charity, but Seton refused any obligation that would interfere with her duties to her children. Consequently, their way of life was flexible, bound by no obligations other than to teach children. Elizabeth resisted intrusions: *she* was mother, principal, teacher, spiritual director, and counselor.

Painfully aware of those who once branded her a heretic, she would not deny admission to members of other religious traditions. Taking responsibility for the instruction of African American children, she rejoiced: "*Excellentissimo!*" Insisting on the education of girls, she must have quashed the pragmatic question: Why should they learn to read when they could help with the plowing?

Financial worries, uncertainty about her children's welfare and the health of her sisters, fleas, food shortages, cold, and constant sickness must have led her to write, "Tribulation is my element." She confided to a friend, "My old heart, made of leather and not to be broken . . . keeps up."

Yet Seton tapped that great mercy, a sense of humor. She lightly dismissed a body of work that would leave most people exhausted, or at least tempted to brag. "A ruined carcass, bundled up in old shawls and flannels, I never do the least work of any kind." Her arrival in Emmitsburg was historic for American Catholics, but she describes it tongue-in-cheek: "The dogs & pigs came out to meet us, and the geese stretched their necks in mute demand to know if we were any of their sort, to which we gave assent."

And the circles continued to expand: from the original foundation at Emmitsburg to Philadelphia and New York. Eventually, a decision to include the children of the wealthy resolved financial problems. Seton envisioned her students spreading over cities like good leaven. The work she began would eventually touch soldiers on Civil War battlefields, AIDS patients in Haiti, and children learning to read in Peru or Taiwan. Her hope that she sowed "the seed of an immensity of future good" proved accurate.

Even at the end of her life, she remained the mother, confessing that her sons caused her the most anxiety. Each time she received bad news of them, she'd sigh, "What's a mother to do but pray and dote?" She wrote them once, "You two boys are the whole world to me." The evening of her death, she checked to make sure that the children in the poor school had enough for dinner. My friend Carol would understand: at her core, Elizabeth Ann Seton was a nurturing mom.

The Portrait

The cabin in the background looks like all the Lincoln-log constructions of our childhoods. The rawness of frontier life becomes vivid when Seton describes shoveling snow off the beds in the morning. Not visible in the pine forest are the white palings surrounding her two daughters' graves. She writes of looking twenty times a day at the "little woods where my darlings sleep." Her eyes draw the reader—that penetrating gaze that an onlooker noticed at Seton's deathbed: "Her eyes so expressive, the look that pierces Heaven."

One might expect that on her slate she'd list the unpaid bills or outline the next scheme to make money. For someone struggling to feed and educate fifty kids in an isolated area, a grocery list is expected more than this bolt from the blue. Yet the chalked message in the neat penmanship is typical, "We must be careful to meet our Grace."

She speaks from experience. She had met her Grace in husband and children, sacrament and story, friends and relatives, sisters and students. She knew what she was talking about.

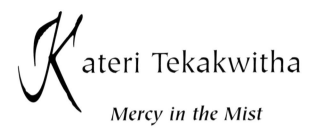

Kateri Tekakwitha

Mercy in the Mist

Visit the sick

They came expecting savages. Instead they found saints. Seventeenth-century French explorers and clergy comment often on the dignity and discipline of Native Americans. These rumors of sanctity culminated in one person who embodied the best of both Native American and Christian traditions: Kateri Tekakwitha. She holds both flute and cross to symbolize the two.

The piney mists of northern forests and legend swirl around her, so we may never know the real person as well as we do some of the other merciful women who left books or photographs behind. Her testimony comes from others and is celebrated today in the environmental movement, which preserves the woods and streams where she liked to contemplate. Knowing how environmentalists respect the balance of nature, fight for its purity and beauty, and defend endangered species, we can intuit something of Kateri.

Her Biography

The biographical facts are sparse: her father, a respected Mohawk chief, came from a matrilineal family, so he was accustomed to women taking leadership. Kateri's mother was an Algonquin and a Christian. Her parents and her little brother were killed in the smallpox epidemic of 1660, which left her pock-marked and half blind. Her uncle, elected to leadership of the Mohawk people, adopted her. His continued generosity reflected the clan's founding documents, which emphasized care of the orphaned, the weak, and the aged.

Jesuit missionaries to the Mohawk community were impressed by its work of mercy. Despite the fact that their predecessors had been slain, the priests returned to a people they loved. The first, Father Pierron, could not speak the language, but painted vivid scenes on linen. Like the art in this book, his pictures conveyed the truths he was trying to teach. His skills and imagination tapped into native traditions.

When a second Jesuit, skilled in languages, came to Kateri's village, he expanded on previous missionary work by appealing to the people's elegant use of oratory. When they heard Christian songs and images in their own tongue, the Mohawk people were impressed by their clarity and beauty. Furthermore, the people were drawn to the Christmas crib, surrounded by fir boughs. Kateri was especially sensitive and asked for baptism when she turned twenty.

Because of her prominence in the clan, many people came to the celebration of that sacrament in a chapel festively decorated with feathers, ribbons, flowers, and beads. In a wonderful link to another woman of mercy, she was named for Catherine of Siena. For Kateri, conversion meant a plunge into mysticism. The beauty of nature, which she had always loved, took on a new intensity because she knew the creator. God drew as close as light rippling on leaves or snow mantling firs.

The Mohawks, however, could not accept Kateri's conversion and ridiculed her. She endured a painful period of gossip and hostility because her people could not understand her new way of life. Eventually she made a long journey on foot to the Sault mission, where she could live among other Native American Christians. The Jesuit who sent a letter of introduction to pastors there wrote, "I send you a treasure, guard it well."

Her Character

Early French biographers use key words to describe her: "*esprit solide*" and "*gaite*." The solidity came from her refusal to believe in dreams but instead to practice unglorious service. She nursed the sick and dying with remarkable cheerfulness, considering that her own health was precarious. Her joy became so contagious that the children were drawn to her for storytelling. She enjoyed ordinary pastimes such as singing and needlework done with a quill on leather, decorating moccasins. At her burial there was no mourning, only public rejoicing.

Her role as spiritual leader was unique because Kateri remained unmarried, unprecedented for one with her prestige as daughter and niece of a chief. Relatives begged her to marry, following the custom of "the other girls." Her adopted sister laid a heavy guilt trip on her, saying that she might not be able to continue Kateri's support and threatening her with poverty. (How many Merion Mercy students have felt the pressure to "be beautiful/have a boyfriend/act like the others"?)

Kateri's friend Marie Therese had a reputation for drunkenness and eccentricity, but her sordid past had given her a sense of God's prodigious mercy. The two became close companions and observed the hospital and teaching sisters of Montreal. There was no precedent for Iroquois religious sisters, so they did not ask for admission to a community.

Instead, they continued their life of prayer together, promising never to marry. Years later, the poet Kathleen Norris would intuit a broader, symbolic meaning of Mary's virginity and that of all women like Kateri and Marie Therese.

I suspect that Mary's "yes" to her new identity, to the immense and wondrous possibilities of her new and holy name may provide an excellent means of conveying to girls that there is something in them that no man can touch; that belongs only to them, and to God.

Norris continues: only as one is at home in herself can she be hospitable to others. "This difficult balance is maintained only as one remains virgin, cognizant of oneself as valuable, unique, and undiminishable at core."[1]

Her Sanctity

While we can understand Kateri only in retrospect, there is no doubt that she was highly respected among her own people. She longed for contemplation and often prayed in the forest, its green depths framing this portrait. But she also delighted in more traditional liturgy.

Her community's chapel became the long-house for God. There Kateri showed the hallmark of holiness: people wanted to be around her. Father Cholenec, an early missionary, records that all the Native Americans liked to be near her, so they could pray better.

It is a tribute to her community that they set aside envy of her holiness to express genuine respect. While her physical penances may seem extreme to us, they were understandable within her culture. Inevitably she had her critics, but in general her people concurred: "One of their flesh and blood and with their ways had very visibly gone to the Christian Paradise and made it their Paradise."[2] Within one young woman, the terrible hostilities between peoples were resolved. Our era desperately needs her peacemaking, her sense of the earth's sacredness, and her tender nursing.

Frances Cabrini

Mercy in Motion

Give drink to the thirsty

My friend Rosa stirs the pasta with the same vigor she plays the piano. She exudes warmth, cooks often, and parties whenever possible. The encouragement *"Mange bene"* (eat lots) rang throughout her childhood and now blesses her own table. The family includes thirty-eight cousins, who happily show up for holiday dinners. That expansive, unruly crowd means the world to her. The most important item on her calendar isn't the business meeting or the inspiring talk she'll give—it's the family vacation.

Rosa's gutsy spirit carries over to the prostitutes, criminals, drug addicts, and alcoholics she works with daily. Calling a hardened criminal "babe," she encourages the woman's progress toward a GED. Quietly, she confides her method: "It's like teaching first grade. We all need a pat on the back." Rosa organizes "Project Bedtime Story" for moms in prison. They read books on tape to their children; she then mails tape and book to the child who delights in mama's voice.

Italianista

Knowing Rosa helps me understand a word that recurs in descriptions of Frances Cabrini: *Italianista*. Did I mention that Rosa is Italian? She could be Frances Cabrini's sister. Although Cabrini Americanized her original name, Francesca, her sisters continued to call her by the Italian endearment La Madre. Cabrini's letter to the prisoners of Sing Sing addressed them as "*Miei buoni amici*" (my dear friends). The same generous spirit that characterizes Rosa marks this saint whose arms embrace a basket brimming with grapes. Even today, she is warmly remembered by the grandchildren of those who knew her.

As a young woman in Italy, she was rejected by two religious communities because of poor health. Her bishop, knowing of no missionary order for women, asked, "Why don't you start one?" Cabrini didn't miss a beat, answering, "I'll look for a house." After she was sent to the United States by Pope Leo XIII in 1889, the rest is history. Cabrini opened sixty-seven charitable institutions and houses in the United States. This is especially impressive during a time when anti-clericals were shutting down religious works and suppressing entire orders.

Like Rosa, Cabrini was a teacher at heart. When she founded a school in a Newark storefront, the rooms were freezing in winter and suffocating in summer. The children had no desks or chairs, but they flocked to Cabrini's sisters, who spoke their language. Enrollment soared to four hundred because they felt happy and loved. Cabrini made do with one school in an abandoned saloon in the East Bronx, but refused the donation of a house in Los Angeles. With no light and no yard, she called it a prison, not a school for children.

Cabrini's energy epitomized the zealous, thirsty, upward mobility of the Italian immigrant. A daunting body of work began with *her* initiative. Unlike other founders, she wasn't asked to start a sisterhood that followed clerical models. So she had a freedom—and a responsibility—few others had. Without a master plan, her work grew from a small orphanage and school in New York City in 1889 to a national network of educational, medical, and social service institutions. A tough business woman, shrewd about contracts, she was tired of swindlers and contractors trying to cheat nuns.

Driven by multiple demands, Cabrini could never do enough for the Italian immigrants. Her heart went out to the many children abandoned when their parents' hopes of instant wealth in the new country didn't materialize. Thirst of all kinds was constant: always too many requests for too few resources. Lack of staff must have broken her heart, because it meant she couldn't meet all the needs.

Her sisters served as interpreters in hospitals and legal proceedings. A Catholic chaplain in Oregon admitted that the sisters who visited prisons could do more good in one visit than he could do in a month. When Italians were thrown out of churches because they didn't dress well or tithe, Cabrini invited them to her community chapel.

From this vantage point, her work seems to have met with saintly success, but the realities were overwhelming need, ethnic prejudice, poor health, difficult travel, vast poverty, recalcitrant clergy, and tension with the Irish and warring factions within the Italian community. Despite her fear of water and seasickness, she made an Atlantic crossing annually for thirty years.

Often finding themselves "without a penny in the house," the sisters would resort to begging. Sometimes the clergy would fail to provide the housing they needed or the right equipment to care for the sick or teach the children. The sisters often heard reproaches that must have stung: "It would be better to go back home." "You're only taking care of a few dirty Italians."[1]

Whirlwind of Activity

Like any mama of a large clan, Frances Cabrini never paused. Biographers record her constant motion: chatting with the sick in the pharmacy, personally selecting the livestock for an Illinois farm, checking the chicken coop, loosening the soil with a pick for a new building in Seattle. She once rode horseback up a mountain for the best vantage point on a property. As Cabrini concluded a contract with bankers, the lawyers were astonished at how astutely she handled the deal. Smiling, she whispered to her sisters, "Poor things, they cannot believe that we are able to do a little business."

Driving Motivation

It is difficult to know much about Frances's inner life. In fact, she tried to conceal it. The journals in which she recorded her spirituality were not for publication. Unlike Dorothy Day, Frances was not primarily a writer. Her energies flowed into the work, the best testament to her. We do, however, get a few glimpses of her motivation. As we have seen with other women, she knew that God's mercy poured through her. Her favorite quotation was, "I can do all things in Him who strengthens me" (Phil. 4:13). She encouraged her sisters, "Hurry—God will do great things!" Cabrini struggled with English, but when asked by a reporter in Los Angeles how she managed her huge network, she commented charmingly, "Oh, I put it all in the Sacred Heart and then I don't get the headache."

As she looks from her portrait through clear black eyes, Cabrini appears serene. But she did not achieve that tranquility easily. She wrote in her journal about her depression:

"My God, what sadness!" and "Neither in God nor my superiors do I find the comfort I need for my soul." But something in her gaze holds the reader and asks without judgment: "Are you living as fully as possible with whatever God gave you? Are you meeting the need and cherishing the harvest?"

In Brother Mickey's image of Frances, the starkness of the black habit contrasts against cascading grapes. That image represents two themes of her life: the privations of poverty and disease, and the abundant, overflowing joy and juice of God. One line from her retreat notes expresses the latter theme: "Give me a heart as big as the universe!"

Lacking much insight into her inner life, we learn about Cabrini from her work. She literally swept the house—after negotiating a real estate contract in Los Angeles, she helped prepare a house for the sisters by sweeping the floors and polishing the furniture. Few women of her day traveled as extensively or acted as powerfully in a male-dominated world. With little or no government funding, sisters were financially responsible for all their hospitals, schools, and orphanages. In 1916, Cabrini even tried a little placer mining in Colorado, hoping to find enough gold to finance the Denver orphanage.

It is appropriate that Frances Cabrini and Katharine Drexel stand together in this portrait. They met in 1915, and Cabrini advised the Philadelphian how to get her order's rule through the intricate process of Roman approval. It's easy to imagine the dramatic duo sipping merlot and having an animated conversation about helping the marginalized. By the time they finished the bottle, Cabrini might be smiling, pocketing a check from Drexel.

Afterwards

Today the work of Cabrini's community, the Missionary Sisters of the Sacred Heart, continues in many ways. One example is the Cabrini Mission Corps, laypeople who serve society's neediest members. Another is the Cabrini Medical Center in New York, a 499-bed teaching hospital dedicated to the elderly, the poor, and AIDS patients.

Both Frances and my friend Rosa meet the acid test of holiness. Even under pressure, they are warm, supportive, good-humored, and willing to do anything for a friend. Pass the wine and pasta!

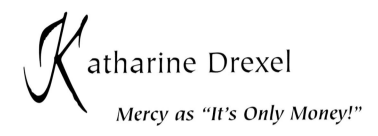Katharine Drexel

Mercy as "It's Only Money!"

Give drink to the thirsty

My friend is wealthy in subtle ways. Her unchipped china matches. Her hair is coiffed, not cut; her nails are manicured, not filed. Real art hangs on her walls. A housekeeper and a gardener maintain her lovely home and garden. She reads a menu left to right; her clothes are impeccably tailored. And yet I do not hate her, nor even—much—envy her.

Why? She never flaunts her wealth and gives much of it away. While she could be spending her days on shopping sprees or in golf games, she volunteers at an inner-city school. Because she lacks pretension, her children are unspoiled.

Adored Daughter

This friend gives me insight into Katharine Drexel. Her mother died a month after her birth, and she was raised by her father and stepmother, Emma Bouvier. Their home had a strong religious sense, where praying was like breathing. Katharine's parents believed their wealth belonged to God; they were entrusted to share it with the poor.

Katharine's father ran the largest investment house in the world at the time, and this powerful, successful man took his daughter with him on trips from their Philadelphia home to the west. There, as a young girl, she saw the horrifying living conditions of Native Americans. When she donated $100 from her clothing budget to a Tacoma settlement church, she was afraid to tell her father. But when she told, he congratulated her, "It's the right thing to do, Katie." The child's instinct was just the beginning.

As an adolescent, Katharine seemed unimpressed with her wealth. She dismissed her social debut, which must have cost a bundle, as "attending a little party." When she and her two sisters vacationed at the shore, her father warned, "I hope you are careful not to get into deep water either with the beaux or the surf." Her portrait here suggests the poise, confidence, and generosity of the girl who offered a brimming cup gladly and graciously.

Emma developed cancer when Katharine was twenty-four. Nursing her, the young woman realized that none of the family fortune could save her stepmother. On her father's death, Katharine inherited $14 million, which would equal roughly $200 million today. She didn't spend this staggering amount on European trips, shoes, or lavish homes. Philadelphia was teeming with immigrants, and the Catholic Church responded with a network of schools, hospitals, and orphanages—all good causes that requested her help. Yet the young heiress looked beyond the church, beyond the social services everyone else provided.

Drexel realized that no one was doing anything for the education of African Americans and Native Americans, and she grieved for the neglect and indignities they suffered. She began to pour her fortune into their cause and to recruit

European missionaries. But eventually she asked herself a tough question, Why do you send others and not go yourself?

Inner and Outer Struggle

There ensued an inner struggle between Katharine's ideals and her wariness of a vowed religious life. She'd never been without luxury and dreaded the "old maidish dispositions" of the convent, the poverty, the thought of never being alone. Yet her whole dilemma came down to one question: What can I do for God's greater glory and service?

She waged an external battle with her mentor, Bishop O'Connor, who opposed her becoming a nun. We get only a hint of the steeliness in the erect girl holding the chalice. In letters to O'Connor she asked, "What can I desire better than this?" "Will Our Lord at the day of judgement condemn me for approaching as near to Him as possible?" "Are you afraid to give me to Christ?" Given her final decision, "I am not obliged to submit my judgement to yours," it shouldn't surprise anyone that the bishop capitulated.

The Bold Adult

If anyone is deluded that mercy is soft or sentimental, Katharine Drexel shows its efficient, business-like strength. Unable to find a congregation that did the kind of work she wanted, Katharine founded her own. At thirty-three, she took final vows as a Sister of the Blessed Sacrament. Then her passionate commitments and her overarching mercy became vividly apparent. She devoted her energies to One whom Sister Edith Prendergast describes: "Jesus is what we know in our hearts God must surely be . . . loving on the other side of every boundary, every fracture."

The situation for African Americans in the early 1900s hadn't changed much since the days of slavery. Although black people were eager for freedom, they had little education and found few jobs. "Nothing is too good for my students!" vowed Katharine, who saw an education permeated with Christian principles as vital equipment. Starting schools for black girls, she incurred the wrath of the Ku Klux Klan. They burned a cross on her front lawn in 1926 and called her community "nigger sisters."

Despite the racists who targeted her, Katharine continued to buy property and insisted that African Americans should have not only trade schools but academic colleges. But even her abundant charm couldn't convince homeowners righteously defending their neighborhoods. Unfazed, she contributed $750,000 toward the founding of Xavier University in New Orleans, the first Catholic college in the United States for African Americans. She explained her independence: "You have no time to occupy your thoughts with . . . consideration of what others will think. Your business is simply, 'What will my Father in heaven think?'"

All Around Me, Beauty

Drexel's audacity extended to the southwest, where she founded schools in New Mexico and Arizona, vowing, "Don't tell me Indians aren't smart!" Apparently being in the middle of nowhere, not knowing the language didn't bother her. She persisted even through a socialite's worst nightmare, "a party where no one came." Navajo parents were initially reluctant to let their children attend schools far from home. But when the parents were allowed to stay with the students for several weeks, they were finally persuaded of her schools' benefits.

The government schools at the time were intent on turning Navajos into little Americans, obliterating their native culture. Drexel took a different approach, creating a U.N. of different tribes at St. Catherine's school. The sisters never forced their students to deny their culture, but incorporated it with their training in manual arts and prayer. Eventually, the sisters, who seemed oddly dressed and did not speak native languages, grew in their appreciation of the southwest, its peoples, its beauty. Mercy flourished as diverse groups learned to communicate and work together.

Within four years, Drexel had established thirteen Native American schools. Their graduates form a network now, many in leadership positions. Furthermore, she donated over a million dollars to the Bureau of Catholic Indian Missions, and $100,000 a year to support schools on the reservations. She traveled extensively to visit them and kept careful records of her keen, business-like observations. Even when she developed typhoid fever, she commented wittily that it hadn't been in her plans, so it must have been in God's.

The Retiree

Another unwelcome development came in 1935. A severe heart condition forced Katharine into retirement, her activity turned to prayer. Giving up travel and work, she spent the last twenty years of her life in reflection. She maintained extensive correspondence, but serenely traded a vast arena for a small infirmary. Looking back without regret, she wrote with wonder: "God has let me see with my own eyes the good results of God's desire." Indeed, her accomplishments are magnificent: over two hundred institutions serving twenty-five thousand African Americans and Native Americans.

Katharine had always operated without fanfare, but the fiftieth anniversary of her order prompted a big celebration. Pueblo and Navajo students danced in costume. The Xavier University Music Department performed scenes from the opera *Carmen* and numerous glee clubs sang. One Native American praised Katharine's vision of "what you and I could be." In time, she received so many honorary doctorates that she joked, "Oh, I am a lot of doctors now!"

The Saint

Katharine Drexel was more than that. The process of canonization is usually tedious, expensive, and long, but for Drexel, it came unusually fast: only forty years after her death in 1955. As tribute to Katharine's broad sympathies and creative range, Native Americans danced at her beatification. The somber halls of the Vatican rang with rare drums and stomping feet; the solemnity was graced with feathers and beads. Katharine Drexel, the joyful lover of the arts, might have smiled in appreciation. As Native Americans say, "It is finished in beauty."

$\mathcal{J}$osephine Bakhita
Mercies Great and Small

Forgive injuries

If I were sobbing with heartbreak, bitter with rage, seething after a betrayal, I would come to her. She would hold me in her arms. She would understand. Her hands are as comforting as warm wool mittens; her skin is mocha. I could get lost in the deep wells of her eyes. The eyes say it all: "Look what happened to me. I survived. I'm not bitter."

Few people know her story, but she should not go unsung. "Survivor" is a glib term tossed about on reality TV shows, but Josephine gives the word new meaning. Born in 1869, she was captured by slave traders at the age of nine. They gave her the nickname Bakhita, which meant "lucky." But she felt far from fortunate.

Tragic Saga

Her captors once beat her to unconsciousness. She was left half-dead for over a month. But the worst torture came from a Turkish general's wife. It was customary to tattoo slaves because it increased the prestige and profits to their masters when they were sold. Josephine had to watch as a friend endured this process. Then Josephine was pinned to the ground by her hands and feet. The witch cut her with a razor in over sixty places. Salt was rubbed into the cuts because it would prevent healing and leave more visible scars. Josephine experienced this sustained, excruciating pain before she turned fourteen.

Her only comment? "I thought I would die." Bathed in blood, she was left on a mat for three months, unable to move, without a kind word or a cloth to wipe her wounds. Finally, mercifully, the story improves. Josephine was sold in the Khartoum market to an Italian diplomat and accompanied their child to school in Italy. She learned the Christian religion from the Sisters of Charity of Canossa and it changed her life dramatically.

Ordered to return to Africa with the family because she was considered their property, she refused. The stunning audacity of the former slave broke the chains she holds in this portrait. She explained, "I can't risk losing God."

Resurrection

The ensuing battle was finally resolved by diplomatic negotiations: since slavery was illegal in Italy, Josephine was free. Discovering a crucifix with a man on it both suffering and loving intensely, she recognized a kindred spirit. Intrigued by Christianity with its Father God and Mother Mary, who resembled the parents she mourned, Josephine was baptized.

"Here I became a daughter of God," she said. So that's what a child of God looks like. No wonder just being near her portrait feels prayerful. Maybe that explains the comfort in her face, the giant heart in her small stature. Brutally traumatized before most girls get a driver's permit, she could never stop marveling that she was important in God's eyes.

With that assurance, Josephine could forgive the scars she bore on her body. At age forty-one, she joined the convent, where she was happy as cook, seamstress, and doorkeeper. She told her sisters, "You teach catechism. I'll stay in the chapel and pray that you teach well."

Her portrait colors are black and brown, nothing flashy like lime or flamingo. Steadily, she survived two world wars and became known throughout Italy. To children who had never met an African, she reassured: "I'm made of chocolate!" She was known as Madre Moretta, the Black Mother, revered by both Italians and Africans. Her speaking tours throughout Italy raised support for the missions.

But it was the ordinary kindnesses that drew people to her. She became a fine chef and warmed the plates in winter to make sure her dishes arrived hot and tasty. Her attitude to her Arab captors was, "Poor things! They did not know God." Her sweetness soothed children, the poor, and the sick. But she once challenged a group of seminarians, "Become saints, for God's sake!"

So how do you learn to forgive enormous wrongs? You spend time with someone like her. You live beneath the gaze of those black-brown eyes. You linger within the affirmation of that wise half-smile. And you get a hint of what grace can do, what wrongs mercy can mend.

Thea Bowman

Sung Mercy

⁓

Feed the hungry

Ask any Discman-wearing student at Merion Mercy Academy how long she could live without music. Her look of consternation would answer eloquently. Music for driving, for studying, for dancing: a land without music would be a still and silent country. Ask her mother the same question, and she might describe her exercise class, where music slides over sore muscles, relaxes creaky joints, and lifts droopy spirits.

The student's grandmother may have benefited from a headset in the dentist's chair, where music distracts attention even from a root canal. Harpists now accompany the dying until they have reached beyond the last plucked notes. Song feeds the spirit as surely as abundant biscuits nourish the body.

Thea Bowman enriches and expands these uses of music. If mercy has a voice, it is hers. Soft as suede, strong as oak, Thea's song nurtured countless people with merciful tones. She called her songs bonfires, sure as the smell of a fish fry, calling folks out of their chilly nights. In this portrait, she cradles her microphone as some would hold a ladle, stirring a flavorful stew.

Here she is lady of the turban, dressed in vivid African patterns the tropical colors of melons and jungles. Music fills the air around her. Yet a profound stillness also hovers about her, a contemplation underlying all she does.

The First Notes

Thea turned to the mercy of song throughout her lifetime, but must have found it especially consoling when she became a Catholic at age ten. She then left her Mississippi home at sixteen to become the only African American member of the Franciscan Sisters of Perpetual Adoration. In her move to La Crosse, Wisconsin, she left not only southern warmth but the rich matrix that had formed her.

How painful that must have been is only dimly suggested when she wrote later: becoming Catholic in the forties meant leaving behind "the music that was an expression of the spirituality of our home, community and upbringing." One biographer smiles, remembering the way Thea bundled up for cold climates. She took his grandmother's advice: "In the winter if you have to choose between being pretty and being warm, choose warm."[1]

Link to the Legacy

But Thea Bowman would not leave her cultural base forever. As she reclaimed her musical heritage, she became for African Americans the link to their past, their treasured legacy. Before Thea, black Catholics were expected to give up singing their spirituals, dancing, and testifying in the spirit because those were suspiciously "Protestant" customs.

As a tremendous mercy to her people, Thea affirmed the black Catholic identity. She shaped it through the Institute of Black Catholic Studies at Xavier University, New Orleans, which she helped found in 1980. Furthermore, she mercifully shared the heritage with people of other cultures, who learned from black Catholics the importance of family, community, celebration, and a tradition of survival and resistance.

She taught African Americans that their birthright was a poignant well of suffering and resurrection. The songs of slavery had taught her people that no grave is ever final. Survivors of exile, callous and inhuman treatment, almost unendurable pain, they knew in their bones the experiences that prompted their spiritual: "Sometimes I feel like a motherless child . . . sometimes I feel like I can't go on, a long ways from home."

Thea knew the heartbreak of lullabies sung to black children who cried alone outdoors while their mothers cared for white children inside a mansion. When the mother couldn't hold or cradle her child, her song reached out to rock and comfort.[2]

Songs like Thea's bridged from times of slavery to the contemporary civil rights movement. Facing the dogs, the hate-filled violence, and the fire hoses, the marchers sang "We Shall Overcome." As Joseph Brown, S.J., points out, they didn't mean they would overcome in the next life. They weren't looking to pie in the sky. They meant right here, right now, we'll overcome our own fear of death and our own hesitance to forge a just path for our children. For their descendants, that song recalls the powerful memory of the freedom riders and protesters. As a tribute to Thea Bowman, the American bishops at her prompting linked arms and sang it again in 1989.

African American spirituality speaks powerfully to people of all cultures because it so vividly expresses the wilderness of exile and the sweetness of deliverance. That it does so in song is its particular genius. Tears are mingled with joyous notes because song can articulate pain and yearning "too high, too low, too wide, too deep for words."[3]

Frederick Douglass noted the irony of some slaveholders using their slaves' singing as proof that they were happy. Instead, he points out, slaves sing most when they're miserable. "The songs of the slave represent the sorrows of his heart; and he is relieved by them . . . as an aching heart is relieved by its tears."

The tradition stretched back to the horrors of the mid-Atlantic passage, when one slave groaned her pain and another slave, chained to someone else, answered. "Two souls joined together in the lowest pit of hell started to climb back up to their humanity."[4]

Broadening the African American experience of oppression to all people who have been dehumanized, Catherine Hilkert describes their transformation: "A share in God's own heart stretched the human heart to the point where both women and men chose to lay down their lives for their friends."[5]

Melody in Prayer

African Americans knew themselves as biblical people, entering another exodus, singing new psalms. Like the Israelites, they prayed to be so strengthened and transformed by God's presence that the world with its evil, oppression, and hostility could not defeat them. Their identification with Moses and Jesus was even more impressive in light of the way religion was used to oppress them and tell them they were evil. Ironically, the system of slavery, intended to break the human spirit, instead produced individuals of magnificent generosity, deep compassion, and uncommon transcendence.

Their sacred song is soulful, full of movement. As Clarence Rivers explains, "That which is unmoved and unmoving is not spiritual, it is dead!"[6] It brings to prayer the immediate reality, whether that is grief or joy, struggle or oppression.

Throughout the stories of merciful women, we have seen an identification with Jesus that echoes in the stories of Thea's people. "They stood at the cross and saw *themselves* hanging in the middle of the air. They saw a Jesus who knew every tear and every heartbreak." Because they themselves had been there, "Even in the face of the unimaginable grief, seeing God hanging from a tree, they could still soothe his dying breath with a song of understanding."[7]

Long before the research was done, this prayerful, singing community knew the truth of a study reported on National Public Radio. Research in Britain measured the difference between people singing in church and in other group settings. They found that song in the worship setting released endorphins that help health. These were not present in any other setting, nor in speaking.

The Finale

After completing her doctorate at the Catholic University of America, Thea punctuated her talks with quotations from Aristotle and Aquinas, interspersed with the bawdy lyrics of

Delta blues. Yet her advanced degree never became a barrier to less educated people.

What a gift Thea gave children, who may feel small and defenseless, to dance them through "Joshua fit the battle of Jericho." Belting out its triumphant chorus, they imagined themselves toppling impenetrable walls. She knew they couldn't feel outnumbered or afraid while singing "and the walls come tumbling down!"

Diagnosed with breast cancer in 1984, Thea died six years later at the age of fifty-three. In her final illness, she gave herself the mercy of song: clinging to a song alleviated the pain. "Sometimes when the pain got so bad . . . it felt like I was being turned inside out like you would pull off a glove, I could hear a song in my head, and I could hold on to the song for just a little rest." "I was able to find some spark within and nurture it long enough with song that the flame could hold the pain at bay."

She proved that song is sacramental: as we hear it or sing it, we feel its healing. Then the song encourages us to get busy with the work of healing, the work of mercy. The singer lifts the people of God to a new plane of understanding and participation. Thea knew this dynamic both intellectually and experientially because it had worked in her own life.

Feeling alone, she could "hear some old lady singing about her Jesus while she's cleaning greens for supper, then you know you belong somewhere, to somebody, and you know you got a home to get to, some day."

Womanist theologian Shawn Copeland explains how in slave narratives written by women, they are not passive victims of suffering. Instead, these active agents take charge of many lives and resist brutality. "These women who held no authority or power in any dominant system nevertheless spoke with authority in creating their own language—the language of sass."[8]

They used sass to protect their self-esteem, speak truth, challenge immorality. Their hope-filled hearts gave their children stories of liberation and promises of freedom. Most important, their example taught how suffering can be transformative. They knew that the way they were treated was an outrage to human dignity and to their creator. Courageously, they passed on life in a culture of death.

Thea Bowman knew the language of sass. How else could she accomplish so much in a racist society, become the heroine of so many young people? She fed them with song and spirit; they gave it right back, singing and dancing with sass.

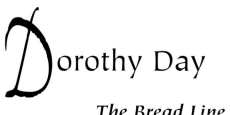

Dorothy Day

The Bread Line of Mercy

Feed the hungry

It seems natural to place Dorothy Day and Thea Bowman together. Each in her own way fed the hungry. Thea would have applauded Dorothy's activism, and Dorothy would have loved Thea's singing. Day's determined stance here shows her conviction. She stands firmly behind the *Catholic Worker* newsletter, just as she would follow a banner into a protest march. Dorothy's prolific writing reveals her character. More than any other merciful woman, she tells her own story.

Life Themes

A vignette from her childhood forecasts the themes of Dorothy Day's life. Her autobiography records how pushing her little brother in his stroller, she chose to walk not in parks but through gray streets, past taverns in poor neighborhoods. There she enjoyed the beauty of tiny flower gardens, vegetable patches, marigolds, the smells of good bread and roasting coffee. There she forecast her future, discovering "enough beauty to satisfy me."

Poverty and beauty: the two are intertwined throughout Day's life. As an adult she would live in the slums, tenements, and hospices of Washington, Baltimore, New York, Milwaukee, with the unemployed, the sick, the addicted. In his introduction to *The Long Loneliness*, Daniel Berrigan strings it like a litany: "She wrote from Cuba, from Rome, from jail, from the fields of the migrant workers, from coal mining areas, from the reservations of the far West. In her travels she lived with, talked with, ate with, walked miles with, marched with; she became the guardian angel of the unangelic, a very angel of 'with.'"

Early Inspirations

The process of coming to spiritual illumination was slow and fitful, but it is telling that one of Day's favorite quotations came from Dostoevsky's novel *The Possessed*: "All my life I have been haunted by God." In her youth, she was drawn by beauty, asking her common-law husband, Forster Batterham, "How can there be no God, when there are all these beautiful things?" One biographer comments, "From her childhood, Day had a marked capacity for awe and a vulnerability to beauty."[1]

What finally brought her into the Catholic faith was the birth of her daughter, Tamar. Because of a previous abortion, Day thought she was unable to conceive, so the child was a delightful surprise. As one of the few mothers among the merciful women, she brings unique insights on the maternal dimensions of mercy. "No human creature could receive or contain so vast a flood of love and joy as I often felt after the birth of my child. With this came the need to worship, to adore."

Tamar's middle name came from another woman of mercy: Teresa of Avila. Day "fell in love with her" because Teresa liked novels, wore a bright red dress when she entered the convent, and had a faith so durable she could tease God. "Very female, very stormy, very valiant. . . . Nothing to disturb or affright us except, perhaps, vermin in uncomfortable inns."

In this community of spiritual mentors, Thérèse of Lisieux's autobiography taught Day "the little way," which she followed even in prison. Day wrote of her, "the significance of our smallest acts! . . . The significance of the little things we leave undone! The protests we do not make, the stands we do not take, we who are living in the world."

Her conversion to Catholicism, early commitment to the poor, and choice of mentors inspired her initially. But Dorothy still prayed for direction. As a young woman, she knew few adult Catholics and felt that journalism (her profession) simply wasn't enough. She wanted to do more. Her prayer for help was answered in the person of Peter Maurin.

Peter didn't begin with negatives: tearing down structures or painting an intense picture of injustice. Instead, he empowered people. "He aroused in you a sense of your own capacities for work, for accomplishment. He made you feel that you and all men had great and generous hearts with which to love God." He liked to call himself "a troubadour of Christ, singing solutions to the world's ills." He inspired Dorothy with his "vision of a society where it is easier . . . to be good."

The Gritty Work

But the visionary Maurin relied on Day for the practicalities. With his inspiration, she began the *Catholic Worker* newspaper, soup kitchens, and houses of hospitality. Probably neither one anticipated the unsanitized realities the work entailed. Ever pragmatic, Dorothy later wrote about Peter, "Every now and then I'd look at him and groan, 'why did you have to start all this anyway?'"

"All this" meant constant crisis, impossible odds. The Catholic Worker house meant: "daily collisions with human need and suffering . . . fights on the [bread] line, injuries, sickness, mental breakdowns, drunkenness, clashing personalities, ideological combat, hysterical or despairing individuals, empty bank accounts, theft or destruction of property, fires, evictions, demands from the city for costly alteration of buildings, withdrawal of co-workers to other places, and the interventions of death." Day was the final arbiter of conflict within the Catholic Worker movement and often its financial support. Her books were written "so the bills will be paid for a very big family."

"The work is as basic as bread," she wrote. In the

city's squalor, she relied on God to multiply loaves and fishes. Despite shaky financial arrangements, she continued to feed the poor, edit and print the newsletter, house the homeless, and care for the sick. Retrieving canned goods with stained labels, she explained, "you can feed many hungry people by such means. The immediate solution will always be the works of mercy."

Her text and inspiration was Matthew 25: "Only the gospel words about the corporal works of mercy . . . have kept us going all these years." While she was the most vocal and visible advocate of the Catholic Worker movement, Day considered it a community project: "A community was growing up. A community of the poor, who enjoyed being together, who felt that they were embarked on a great enterprise, who had a mission. All of them understood the works of mercy."

Day is more explicit about the works of mercy than the other women profiled here. She even broadened them to include protesting discrimination in housing or the draft. "When we were invited to help during a strike we went to perform the works of mercy, which include not only feeding the hungry, visiting the imprisoned, but enlightening the ignorant and rebuking the unjust. We were ready to 'endure wrongs patiently' . . . but we were not going to be meek for others, enduring THEIR wrongs patiently."

Her "manifesto of mercy" came in response to a social worker who asked how long "guests" could stay at the Worker. Day answered, "We let them stay forever. They live with us, they die with us, and we give them a Christian burial. We pray for them after they are dead. Once they are taken in, they become members of the family. Or rather they always were members of the family. They are our brothers and sisters in Christ."

Day's spirituality eventually took on the colorful, practical tone of her life at the Catholic Worker soup kitchen and house of hospitality. When she invited a priest to give talks to the staff, they used the only room they had, frequently filled with sleeping, unemployed construction workers. "We often listened to him to the tune of snoring guests."

Mothering the Child—And the Work

Day's life of faith began with her child and centered on her. "If I had written the greatest book, composed the greatest symphony, painted the most beautiful painting or carved the most exquisite figure, I could not have felt the more exalted creator than I did when they placed my child in my arms."

Despite other sacrifices, Day kept the precious coin: "I had Tamar." She delighted in the little girl who prayed standing on her head, the young woman who kept her laughing, the mother of her grandchildren, and the adult daughter who made her tea and held her hand the afternoon she died. The mother–daughter relationship was vital to all Day's work. When Tamar was a young adult, Day wrote, "She was, of course, everything to me. I have not even to this day ceased to look upon her with wonder."

Another precious coin was the work of the Catholic Worker. As a child, Day had been drawn to the plight of the masses and yearned for spiritual adventure. Her work satisfied that longing and gave her abundant chances to practice the works of mercy daily. Even in jail Dorothy thanked God "for the opportunity to be there, to be stripped of all that the earth holds dear, to share in some way the life of prisoners, guilty and innocent, all over the world."

The growth of the movement, its spread throughout the country must have been deeply gratifying. Looking back on the phenomenon, Day reflected, "It all happened while we sat there talking, and it is still going on." Taking unpopular stands for peace and justice, she accomplished what few women of her day imagined possible in the male-dominated worlds of journalism and church.

Day was also able to approach spirituality with a uniquely hardheaded stance. Asked by a woman hungry for mystical experiences if she had ecstasies and visions, Dorothy replied, "Visions of unpaid bills."

The ultimate treasure was "this terrible, overwhelming, demanding love of the living God." Honest about how much she missed having a husband, Day referred to Dostoevsky's saying: "love in reality is a harsh and dreadful thing compared to love in dreams." Throughout an arduous life, she trusted providence so completely that the symbol of loaves and fishes, which she saw multiplied a hundredfold to feed many, appears on her tombstone.

Cause for Celebration

"What a driving power joy is!" Day declared. Indeed, it drove her to accomplish miracles. During her earliest conversion, she was troubled that she might be falling into what her communist friends called "the opiate of the people." But Day reasoned, "I am praying because I am happy, not because I am unhappy." She came to God not from grief or despair, but in thanks. Day's celebration followed the example of her mentor, Teresa of Avila, who danced with castanets "to make life more bearable," and fed her nuns steak.

Like C. S. Lewis, Day was "surprised by joy." "I found myself, a barren woman, the joyful mother of children." Her joy in Tamar expanded to the whole Catholic Worker family (which she would *never* call an organization or institution). With the constant pressure of grinding poverty, she admitted, "It is not easy always to be joyful, to keep in mind the duty of delight."

Yet she maintained her earliest captivation with beauty, insisting that she spend time away from the city on Staten Island beaches or outlying farms. Her rationale was clear: "If we do not learn to enjoy God now we never will. If we do not learn to praise Him and thank Him and rejoice in Him now, we never will." She wrote of a moonlit night at a farm: "There was a quiet and perfect peace and a happiness so deep and strong and thankful that even my words of prayer seemed inadequate to express my joy."

Day gathered not only friends and neighbors who helped on the newspaper and in soup kitchens: she connected with the whole mystical body. Specifically, she identified with another woman of mercy. "What Catherine of Siena had done in the fourteenth century, Peter believed Dorothy could do in the twentieth. She would 'move mountains and have influence on governments, temporal and spiritual.'"

Throughout her life, she remained free of puffery or pomposity. When she somewhat guiltily devoured a whole fruit salad, the earlier comparison emerged again: "I ate it all! How sensual I am. A glutton. Was it St. Catherine of Siena or St. Angela Foligno who wanted to tie a baked chicken around her neck and run through the streets shouting, 'I am a glutton'?"

Day transcended not only time but distance in her connections with women of mercy. When she visited India, Mother Teresa of Calcutta garlanded her with fresh flowers at the airport. When Day spoke to the Missionaries of Charity there about arrests and jail, they were astonished. They knew Gandhi had done this, but for the first time, they heard protest placed in a Christian context.[2]

Day's international travels resembled those of Frances Cabrini and Teresa of Avila. As she approached the final journey into the next life, Day quoted Teresa again, "The mules are packed, they are kicking, the road will be rocky, but the destination is sure."

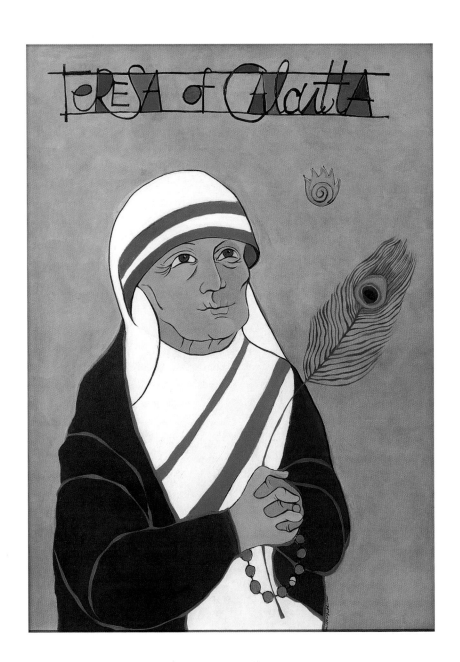

TERESA of Calcutta

Mother Teresa of Calcutta

Mercy as Beauty

Clothe the naked

Sometimes it seems as simple as the pure blue and white lines of her clothing. Mother Teresa and her little band of sisters care for the poor, the dying, the unwanted, and the homeless in the slums of Calcutta. To those who face daily the quagmire of business decisions, tangled relationships, and complex scheduling, her work by contrast seems a clear, uncomplicated following of the gospel.

Yet few of us abandon our routines, don saris, and join the movement in India. Perhaps we want to believe that something of Teresa's spirit can invigorate our lives; some of her clarity can penetrate our shadows; some of her compassion can move through us to those we touch each day. Our contacts may not be as naked and diseased as those Teresa cared for, but they have the same needs for attention and affection.

Teresa covered the naked with more than cloth, and her work transcends the response to physical need. She taught us to look deeper, to see that the worst suffering wasn't being naked but being unloved. Her life corresponds closely to the gospel parable in the Introduction. As she lights her lamp, sweeps her house, finds the coin and celebrates, she shows us how to bring the mercy of Calcutta's streets into twenty-first-century North America.

Light the Lamp

Teresa apparently had the same luminosity that attracted people to Jesus. Everyone wanted to be near her in life, and after her death she exerts the same attraction. Her biographer, Malcolm Muggeridge, believed that for people who have trouble grasping "Christ's great propositions of love . . . someone like Mother Teresa is a godsend. She is this love in person."[1] This woman of small stature and homely face radiates Christ's love more accessibly than metaphysical or ethical statements.

Like the other women of mercy, she grounded her work in a firm base of spirituality. She holds a rosary because her devotions were traditional. Daily Mass was her "sustenance and strength"; from it she went forth to meet Jesus in needy people. The Jesus she encountered was the same at the altar and in the streets. Mother Teresa contrasted the welfare system with the work of her Missionaries of Charity: welfare is directed to a purpose, but Christian love to a person. Those doing social work did it for something; she did it for *someone*.

As the sisters go into the filth of Calcutta or the slums around the world, they take literally the biblical imperative to let one's light shine for all to see. Mother Teresa's face, shining with love, gave viewers of a BBC documentary about her such a vivid glimpse of the "glorious liberty of God's children" that they responded with a phenomenal outpouring of money—despite the fact that funds were never requested.

"In the slums we are the light of God's kindness to the poor," Teresa declared. A charming anecdote proves the truth of her saying. Cleaning the house for an old man who had a splendid lamp covered with dust, Teresa asked why he didn't turn it on.

"For whom?" the man replied. "No one comes to see me. I don't need the lamp."

"And if the sisters come to see you, will you turn the lamp on?" she asked.

"Yes, if I hear a human voice."

Sometime later the old man sent the message: "Tell my friend that the lamp she lighted in my life is still burning."[2]

Sweep the House

No one was less sentimental or more "earthy" than Mother Teresa. She would engage in lively discussion with beggars about their "take" of the day, explaining that, in a dull routine, "It's interesting for them." If a topic was dear to the heart of the lepers, she would take eager interest in it.

In view of the vast international organization that her efforts have established, it is stunning to remember that she began alone, with several rupees and some abandoned children. A statistic from 1980 says that anywhere between thirty and sixty thousand people came to her house of the dying—with the disclaimer: "Mother Teresa is not the best bookkeeper in the world."[3] She had more important things to worry about, but her basic philosophy shines: "They lived like animals. At least they die like human beings."

She chose to enter situations of such squalor, odor, and raw pain that most of us would run screaming in the opposite direction. In addition to her peacock feather (more on that later), she might also hold a shining bucket, almost the only possession of the sisters. It represents their vigorous work of washing and the other countless chores of caring for unwanted babies, malnourished children, AIDS patients, homeless people, the dying, and lepers.

The constant work of washing, treating, holding, and comforting over and over with limited supplies, resources, and helpers is exhausting. The nuns admit that they live in a state of perpetual fatigue. Teresa herself said, "At times I feel like an empty vessel, a limp rag. I feel so alone, so miserable." Yet even in the heat and humidity of India, she didn't own a fan, asking: "How can I tell the poor 'I love you and understand you,' if I don't live like them?"

One reason Teresa holds the peacock feather is that it is the sacred, national bird of India, where it lives wild. Albanian by birth, she received Indian citizenship in 1948. She was so much a part of her adopted country that she could say, "I'm an Indian, I don't even remember for how many years now. India is my country." Her choice of sari and gesture of bowing with clasped hands are typically Indian.

Yet like Teresa of Avila and Frances Cabrini, she traveled extensively: to Australia, the United States, the Mideast, Asia, Europe—wherever her sisters worked. If one sister had difficulty, she'd fly to her aid. Once when she couldn't afford a plane ticket, she volunteered to be a stewardess! (Indira Gandhi later gave her a free train and plane pass.)

Find the Coin

Another reason she holds the peacock feather is its beauty. Malcolm Muggeridge noticed that "beautiful" was one of Mother Teresa's favorite words. Indeed, she believed her vocation was to be beautiful. That takes on special significance considering that the conditions in which she worked were decidedly unlovely and often downright revolting.

Yet she holds her blue-green plume, radiantly colored like

God's eye. Flannery O'Connor, the novelist who raised pea-
cocks, describes the bird's tail as "a galaxy of gazing, haloed
suns . . . in a green-bronze arch."[4] She observed that people
were struck silent when the fan showing its "little planets"
was fully unfurled. How do we explain the apparent discrep-
ancy with Calcutta's squalor?

Perhaps Mother Teresa had a different angle on beauty
than most people have. One of the most telling examples of
her viewpoint comes in the story of a precariously tiny baby.
Cradling the little mite, Mother Teresa spoke with exaltation:
"See! There's life in her!" She gloried in life-surviving-
against-all-odds as evidence of the divine in our midst. Some
argue with her philosophy, but few question the purity of her
uplifted eyes, the sure stance, the testimony of the work
itself.

In the cry of every abandoned child, she could hear the
child of Bethlehem; in the stumps of the leper she could see
Christ's healing hands. Her touch could bring comfort to the
despairing; her efforts ensured that even the abandoned need
not die alone. Some of her most frequently quoted words
reveal her stance: "To show great love for God and our neigh-

bor we need not do great things. It is how much love we put in the doing that makes our offering something beautiful for God."

Mother Teresa as a still center of beauty: that concept is enfleshed by Muggeridge's experience after putting her on a train at the Calcutta railroad station. When the train pulled away, he felt "as though I were leaving behind me all the beauty and all the joy in the universe."[5] Something of God's shining has rubbed off on her. Seeing photos of her standing beside Princess Diana, a woman with poise, wealth, physical attraction, and international fame, one might find it hard to say who was more beautiful. But the disasters and tragedies of Diana's personal life suggest which woman found the coin.

Celebrate

In the houses of Mother Teresa, the "friends and neighbors" of the parable are multiplying at an astonishing rate. What attracts wealthy and educated young women to a spartan life and harrowing work? Perhaps it is the atmosphere of joy created by people who are clearly happy. Mother Teresa believed that the poor deserved not only service but joy.

Given the rigidity of the Indian caste system, it is hard to imagine girls of the upper classes caring for the untouchables. Yet they flock cheerfully to Mother Teresa for this privilege. Like their God, who delights in clemency (Micah 7:18), they are happy simply to be doing the work. Even in the sticky heat of Bengal, Muggeridge recorded that "the sight of her, or even the thought of her, always gives me a great feeling of happiness."[6]

When Muggeridge asked Teresa about the joyfulness of her sisters as they performed arduous tasks, she replied, "We want to make [the poor] feel that they are loved. If we went to them with a sad face, we would only make them much more depressed." At another time she said, "joy is a net of love in which souls are captured. A heart burning with love is a joyous heart." Modern medicines can now heal leprosy, tuberculosis, and other diseases. But only love can cure the pain of being unwanted.

Like a true Albanian peasant, Mother Teresa loved to joke. When her nuns in Rome were robbed of 40,000 lire, she consoled them: "It's only money. The only thing we have to worry about losing is *you*. And nobody's going to steal you . . . you're much too ugly. Now come along and get to work."[7] Brisk and practical as always.

One final meaning of the peacock symbol is telling. For the first ten centuries of Christianity, the peacock symbolized the resurrected Christ—compassionate, immortal, beautiful. Its golden eyes represented the beatific vision. Like the mythical phoenix in religious art, its flesh did not rot, so it arose eternally. It may seem an imaginative leap from the tiny nun to the gorgeous fan of iridescent feathers. But, given Teresa's beauty, compassion, and identification with Christ, perhaps it's not such a stretch. Perhaps it's the perfect symbol.

Notes

Introduction

1. Mary Catherine Hilkert, *Speaking with Authority: Catherine of Siena and the Voices of Women Today* (Mahwah, N.J.: Paulist Press, 2001), 137.

Mary

1. Gerard Manley Hopkins, "No Worst, There Is None," in *Poems and Prayers of Gerard Manley Hopkins* (Baltimore: Penguin Books, 1956), 61.

2. Gerard Manley Hopkins, "The Virgin Mother Compared to the Air We Breathe," in *Poems and Prayers*, 55.

3. Kathleen Norris, *Meditations on Mary* (New York: Penguin Studio, 1999), 25.

4. Sue Monk Kidd, *The Secret Life of Bees* (New York: Penguin Books, 2002), 288-89.

5. Elizabeth Johnson, *Truly Our Sister: A Theology of Mary in the Communion of Saints* (New York: Continuum, 2003), 267.

6. Sally Cunneen, *In Search of Mary: The Woman and the Symbol* (New York: Ballantine Books, 1996), 193.

7. Joseph Brown, *A Retreat with Thea Bowman and Bede Abram* (Cincinnati: St. Anthony Messenger Press, 1997), 120.

8. Quoted in Cunneen, *In Search of Mary*, 180.

9. Johnson, *Truly Our Sister*, 290.

10. Beatrice Bruteau, *The Easter Mysteries* (New York: Crossroad, 1995), 96-97.

11. Cunneen, *In Search of Mary*, 222, 266, 177.

Mary Magdalene

1. Jane Schaberg, *The Resurrection of Mary Magdalene* (New York: Continuum, 2003), 68.

2. Ibid., 98

3. Ibid.

4. Susan Haskins, *Mary Magdalen: Myth and Metaphor* (New York: Harcourt Brace, 1993), 14-15.

5. Schaberg, *Resurrection of Mary Magdalene,* 9.

6. Price, quoted in Schaberg, *Resurrection of Mary Magdalene,* 232.

7. Ibid., 79.

8. Haskins, *Mary Magdalen,* 13.

9. Ibid, 15.

10. Seim, quoted in Schaberg, *Resurrection of Mary Magdalene,* 338.

11. Ibid., 328, 341.

12. Daniel Boyarin, quoted in Schaberg, *Resurrection of Mary Magdalene,* 349.

Catherine of Siena

1. Bert Ghezzi, *Mystics and Miracles* (Chicago: Loyola University Press, 2002), 31.

2. John Kirvan, *Set Aside Every Fear* (Notre Dame, Ind.: Ave Maria Press, 1997), 12.

3. Ghezzi, *Mystics and Miracles,* 32-33

4. Mary Catherine Hilkert, *Speaking with Authority: Catherine of Siena and the Voices of Women Today* (New York: Paulist Press, 2001), 132.

5. Elizabeth Dreyer, *A Retreat with Catherine of Siena* (Cincinnati: St. Anthony Messenger Press, 1997), 43.

Teresa of Avila

1. Quoted in Kieran Kavanaugh, Introduction to Teresa of Avila, *The Collected Works,* Vol. 2 (Washington, D.C.: ICS Publications, 1980), 23.

2. Kathryn Eastburn, "Beloved: Novelist Toni Morrison to Lec-

ture at Colorado College," *Independent,* Jan. 29-Feb. 4, 2004, quoting a 1981 *Newsweek* interview.

3. Carol Flinders, *Enduring Grace* (San Francisco: HarperSanFrancisco, 1993), 183.

4. Bert Ghezzi, *Mystics and Miracles* (Chicago: Loyola University Press, 2002), 130.

Thérèse of Lisieux

1. Quoted in Paul Elie, *The Life You Save May Be Your Own* (New York: Farrar, Straus & Giroux, 2003), 279, 281.

2. Carol Flinders, *Enduring Grace* (San Francisco: HarperSanFrancisco, 1993), 214.

3. Quoted in Piero Ferrucci, *What We May Be* (New York: Putnam, 1982), 115.

4. Patricia O'Connor, *The Inner Life of Therese of Lisieux* (Huntington, Ind.: Our Sunday Visitor, 1997), 70.

5. Flinders, *Enduring Grace,* 219.

Catherine McAuley

1. M. Bertrand Degnan, *Mercy Unto Thousands: The Life of Mother Mary Catherine McAuley* (Westminster, Md.: Newman Press, 1957), 14.

2. Mary Catherine Hilkert, *Speaking with Authority: Catherine of Siena and the Voices of Women Today* (New York: Paulist Press, 2001), 131.

3. Helen Marie Burns and Sheila Carney, *Praying with Catherine McAuley* (Winona, Minn.: St. Mary's Press, 1996), 23.

4. Ibid., 24.

Elizabeth Ann Seton

1. All Seton quotations are from Ellin Kelly, ed., *Numerous Choirs,* vol. 1, *The Seton Years* (Evansville, Ind.: Mater Dei Provincialate, 1981).

2. Susan Harris, "More Life, More Life: On Parenting," in *The Book of Women's Sermons,* ed. E. Lee Hancock (New York: Riverhead Books, 1999), 142.

Kateri Tekakwitha

1. Kathleen Norris, *Meditations on Mary* (New York: Penguin Studio, 1999), 31-32, 34.
2. Daniel Sargent, *Catherine Tekakwitha* (New York: Longmans, Green, 1936), 244.

Frances Cabrini

1. All Cabrini quotations are from Mary Louise Sullivan, *Mother Cabrini* (New York: Center for Migration Studies, 1992).

Thea Bowman

1. Joseph Brown, *A Retreat with Thea Bowman and Bede Abram* (Cincinnati: St. Anthony Messenger Press, 1997), 7-8.
2. Ibid., 136.
3. Thea Bowman, "The Gift of African American Sacred Song," in *Readings in African American Church Music and Worship*, ed. James Abbington (Chicago: GIA Publications, 2001), 214.
4. Quoted in Brown, *Retreat with Thea Bowman*, 78, 29.
5. Mary Catherine Hilkert, *Speaking with Authority: Catherine of Siena and the Voices of Women Today* (New York: Paulist Press, 2001), 129.
6. Quoted in Bowman, "Gift of African American Sacred Song," 215.
7. Brown, *Retreat with Thea Bowman*, 82, 84.
8. Quoted in Hilkert, *Speaking with Authority*, 122.

Dorothy Day

1. Jim Forest, *Love Is the Measure: A Biography of Dorothy Day* (New York: Paulist Press, 1986), 13.
2. Ibid., 173.

Mother Teresa of Calcutta

1. Malcolm Muggeridge, *Something Beautiful for God* (San Francisco: Harper & Row, 1988), 88-89.

2. Robert Serrou, *Teresa of Calcutta* (New York: McGraw Hill, 1980), 78.

3. Ibid., 50.

4. Flannery O'Connor, "The King of the Birds," in *The Book of Love,* ed. Andrew Greeley and Mary Durkin (New York: Forge Books, 2002), 426.

5. Muggeridge, *Something Beautiful,* 3.

6. Ibid., 18.

7. Serrou, *Teresa of Calcutta,* 118.

Bibliography

Bakhita: From Slavery to Sanctity. Nairobi: Pauline Publications Africa, 2000.

Bowman, Thea. "The Gift of African American Sacred Song." In *Readings in African American Church Music and Worship*, ed. James Abbington. Chicago: GIA Publications, 2001.

Brown, Joseph. *A Retreat with Thea Bowman and Bede Abram*. Cincinnati: St. Anthony Messenger Press, 1997.

Bruteau, Beatrice. *The Easter Mysteries*. New York: Crossroad, 1995.

Bunson, Margaret. *Kateri Tekakwitha: Mystic of the Wilderness*. Huntington, Ind.: Our Sunday Visitor, 1992.

Burns, Helen Marie, and Sheila Carney. *Praying with Catherine McAuley*. Winona, Minn.: St. Mary's Press, 1996.

Cholenec, Pierre. *Catherine Tekakwitha: Her Life*. Hamilton, Ont.: William Lonc, 2002.

Cunneen, Sally. *In Search of Mary: The Woman and the Symbol*. New York: Ballantine Books, 1996.

Day, Dorothy. *The Long Loneliness*. San Francisco: Harper & Row, 1981.

———. *Meditations*. New York: Newman Press, 1970.

Degnan, M. Bertrand. *Mercy Unto Thousands: The Life of Mother Mary Catherine McAuley*. Westminster, Md.: Newman Press, 1957.

Dreyer, Elizabeth. *A Retreat with Catherine of Siena*. Cincinnati: St. Anthony Messenger Press, 1997.

Duffy, Consuela Marie. *Katharine Drexel: A Biography*. Bensalem, Pa.: Sisters of the Blessed Sacrament, 1987.

Elie, Paul, ed. *The Life You Save May Be Your Own*. New York: Farrar, Straus and Giroux, 2003.

———. *A Tremor of Bliss: Contemporary Writers on the Saints*. New York: Harcourt Brace, 1994.

Ellsberg, Robert. *All Saints.* New York: Crossroad, 1998.

Ferrucci, Piero. *What We May Be.* New York: Putnam, 1982.

Flinders, Carol. *Enduring Grace.* San Francisco: HarperSan-Francisco, 1993.

Forest, Jim. *Love Is the Measure: A Biography of Dorothy Day.* New York: Paulist Press, 1986.

Ghezzi, Bert. *Mystics and Miracles.* Chicago: Loyola University Press, 2002.

Gordon, Anne. *A Book of Saints.* New York: Bantam, 1994.

Harris, Susan. "More Life, More Life: On Parenting." In *The Book of Women's Sermons,* ed. E. Lee Hancock. New York: Riverhead Books, 1999.

Haskins, Susan. *Mary Magdalen: Myth and Metaphor.* New York: Harcourt Brace, 1993.

Hilkert, Mary Catherine. *Speaking with Authority: Catherine of Siena and the Voices of Women Today.* New York: Paulist Press, 2001.

Hopkins, Gerard Manley. *Poems and Prayers of Gerard Manley Hopkins.* Baltimore: Penguin Books, 1956.

Johnson, Elizabeth. *Truly Our Sister: A Theology of Mary in the Communion of Saints.* New York: Continuum, 2003.

Kappes, Marcianne. *Track of the Mystic: The Spirituality of Jessica Powers.* Kansas City: Sheed & Ward, 1994.

Kelly, Ellin, ed. *Numerous Choirs,* Volume 1, *The Seton Years.* Evansville, Ind.: Mater Dei Provincialate, 1981.

Kidd, Sue Monk. *The Secret Life of Bees.* New York: Penguin Books, 2002.

Kirvan, John. *Let Nothing Disturb You.* Notre Dame, Ind.: Ave Maria Press, 1996.

———. *Set Aside Every Fear.* Notre Dame, Ind.: Ave Maria Press, 1997.

Muggeridge, Malcolm. *Something Beautiful for God.* San Francisco: Harper & Row, 1988.

Norris, Kathleen. *Meditations on Mary.* New York: Penguin Studio, 1999.

O'Connor, Flannery. "The King of the Birds." In *The Book of Love,* ed. Andrew Greeley and Mary Durkin. New York: Forge Book, 2002.

O'Connor, Patricia. *The Inner Life of Therese of Lisieux*. Huntington, Ind.: Our Sunday Visitor, 1997.

Sargent, Daniel. *Catherine Tekakwitha*. New York: Longmans, Green and Co., 1936.

Schaberg, Jane. *The Resurrection of Mary Magdalene*. New York: Continuum, 2003.

Serrou, Robert. *Teresa of Calcutta*. New York: McGraw Hill, 1980.

Sullivan, Mary Louise. *Mother Cabrini*. New York: Center for Migration Studies, 1992.

Teresa of Avila. *The Collected Works*, Volume 2. Washington, D.C.: ICS Publications, 1980.

Thérèse of Lisieux. *Story of a Soul*. Translated by John Clarke, O.C.D. Washington, D.C.: ICS Publications, 1976.

Wells, Rebecca. *Divine Secrets of the Ya-Ya Sisterhood*. New York: Harper Torch, 2002.

God in the Moment
Making Every Day a Prayer
ISBN 1-57075-578-7

"A hauntingly gorgeous quilt of meditations on prayer." —*Publishers Weekly*

"God works in moments is the old French saying Kathy Coffey uses as the prelude to this down-to-earth and refreshing book on prayer. For the author, our relationship to God can be expressed in a variety of ways. In fact, prayer styles differ according to people's temperaments. A skier gliding down a slope, a cook in the kitchen, a husband holding the hand of his wife, a mother nursing her child, a social worker comforting a lonely person—all of these are 'being prayers.'"
—*Spirituality & Health*

Hidden Women of the Gospels
ISBN 1-57075-477-2

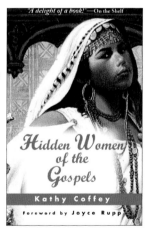

Twenty-one imaginings of behind-the scenes gospel women will inspire and enthrall.
They include:
• A shepherdess who raced to the manger…
• The bride who saw a guest turn water into wine…
• A mother who cooked seven loaves and fishes for her son…
• The waitress who served an extraordinary supper in an upper room…
• A pregnant teen who stood at the foot of a cross…

Soul Sisters
Women in Scripture Speak to Women Today
Edwina Gateley
with art by Louis Glanzman
ISBN 1-57075-443-8

From Mary Magdalene to a Chicago street-walker, from Martha to a contemporary caregiver—moving portraits of women touched by Jesus, then and now.

"In painting and in poetry this book contemplates the women who knew Jesus: our soul sisters if we look deeply enough."
—*Sister Wendy Beckett*

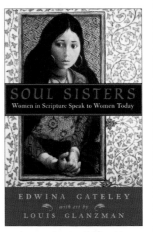

144 pages, paperback
12 full-color paintings

Soul Brothers
Men in the Bible Speak to Men Today
Richard Rohr
with art by Louis Glanzman
ISBN 1-57075-534-5

What do John the Baptist and Jesus have in common with a stockbroker in Manhattan or a seminarian in Brazil? Here are moving portraits of men in the Bible who share more in common with men today than you'd every think!

"Women: give this book to someone you love, but read it for yourself too. It is filled with wonderful insights on what it means to be human." —*Paula D'Arcy, author of* Gift of the Red Bird

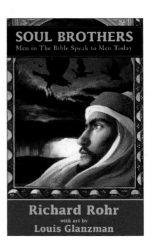

144 pages, paperback
12 full-color paintings

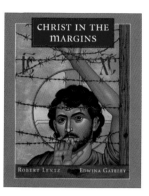